for Matt

THE ENDLESS M

Dustin Hendrick

Enjoy!

Rose Books

While the events described in these essays are all true, some names and identifying characteristics have been fictionalized in order to protect the anonymity of certain individuals and locations.

ISBN 978-1-949745-02-3

For my mothers,
and for Dane

MYSTERY RANCH

The Endless M

Tree trunks, briar patches, handmade fences, dry yellow grass. Hummingbirds shimmer and dance, chittering to each other in great swarms around hanging feeders filled with artificially colored sugar water. The sun returns from behind a passing cloud, casting beams of red and green light through them and onto my face and hands, on the walls of the house. There is commotion inside: a clanking of glass and metal, my grandmother singing Patsy Cline from the kitchen. The box fan above my head rattles in the ill-fitting window frame it has been placed into.

Dogs are sprawled in the grass of the yard, speckled portraits of lethargy, their coats shining in the sun. I am tempted to leave the shade of the porch and go to them, press my face against their upturned sides, feel the accumulated heat there until my cheek burns. But I won't get the chance. The mail carrier, Faye, pulls into the driveway, her boxy red Subaru filled to bursting with envelopes and parcels not yet delivered. She drives her own car to deliver the mail, normal for the time and place: a tiny rural town, safe from the eyes of the fast-moving world sliding up and down the interstate too quickly to notice us. It is 1980. I know nothing else.

This is my first "solid" memory, meaning I know it's something that definitely happened, not a dream or something perhaps seen on television. It was not otherwise altered by the unstable, fluid physics of childhood memory.

1

The dogs are up, even as the car begins to slow, fully awake and surrounding Faye, announcing her arrival in a chorus of happy-barking and raised tails.

My grandmother exits the house into the daylight with a squinting grin. Her face is not yet lined by age and troubles, her hair still black. The damp dish towel in her hands is bordered with fat little owls. She loves owls; they dominate the house's décor in soon-to-be-outdated shades of brown and rusted orange.

"Well, hello, stranger," my grandmother says. Impossible to tell if her joviality is genuine, if she's actually in the mood for company; that's how good she is. Never crack. Never show anything but that smile, that warmth that you wish the world gave back. It never does, not nearly enough for her, but she'll never stop trying.

Faye does not smile. She does not get out of her car. Her face says she'd kill every last dog if she could.

"Hi, Wilma." Her voice is dull, mannish, unintentionally harsh as she greets my grandmother. A long life of work and cigarette smoking has supplanted the original sound of her. She holds out a thin stack of envelopes from her car window, unusual only in that they are already torn open. Two are white. One is piney, Christmas green.

"Looks like he's been writing letters again." Faye tilts her head to where I stand, half in my grandmother's shadow. I feel exposed. It is not the first time I've taken old envelopes from the bureau. It's not the first time I've written secret words on them and placed them in the mailbox across the road, where I'm not supposed to go.

"Oh. It certainly does." My grandmother takes the envelopes and laughs—a clucking, rehearsed sound that says "let it go" to my experienced ear. They are both careful to avoid looking at me. The sun seems no less bright than in the moments before, but the air feels somehow heavier for the exchange.

I wait for the inevitable would-you-like-some-coffee that comes after every car that parks in our driveway. But Faye wastes no time, and my grandmother does not offer. Faye is technically family—a distant relative-in-law of some capacity, like so many who come to call—but some other weight, something I can't see, has overtaken the moment. My grandmother wants her to leave. Her smile doesn't waver, but I know enough of her, even at my age, to know what she's thinking. Her hands are already on my shoulders, gently turning me away from Faye, from the dogs, from the yard and the sun, in the direction of the shaded front porch to the house, where something will be said, but just between the two of us. In private. I know this already. It's how she deals with everything, with everyone.

"You have a good day," Faye says, and if she means it, who can tell? Her eyes, nearly obscured by the photochromic lenses she wears in every memory I have of her, meet mine for an instant. It might be a look of sympathy she gives me, the only pity she's capable of offering. It could be something else entirely. Of course, she would know all about my situation—half relative or not, she will have heard. Word travels at the speed of sound in small towns, in glaring contrast to the slogging slug's pace of everything else. Even the seasons take their time in the farmlands.

Faye's car pulls away, grumbling up the driveway and down the main road, the paved boundary of my existence. The dogs escort her halfway, then return to their lazy posts in the yard. A storm of gold-flecked insects hums in the air above them.

My grandmother leads me into the house by the hand. She seats me on the floral print couch that remains fixed in my memories (it will be gone by the time I start school). She sits across from me in a wicker-backed rocking chair pulled from its home in the corner. I've never seen it moved from that place before. She says nothing, at first, and her eyes do not meet mine. A pall, a white shadow of worry, clouds her kindly features. The sight is enough to pierce my heart.

I look at the envelopes, hanging loosely from my grandmother's sun-burnished hand. Rows of up-and-down lines, like endless chains of *M*'s, zigzag over the printed addresses and images in place of words I don't know how to write, on letters already mailed and opened. A plea written in a nonsensical script known only to me and one other: the woman I tried to send the letters to, hoping she'd know what they meant. The woman whose face remains absent from my earliest memories, though images and sensations come to me in my quieter moments like trails of colored smoke: brown hair and pale blue nightgown on the other side of the bed; a familiar-yet-unfamiliar voice both stern and musical, laughing above me; a crackle of driveway gravel and a wisp of dust like the small line drawn to mark the end of a chapter.

My grandmother sees me watching back and smiles, quickly, but too late. I've seen past the mask, if only for a moment. She was afraid of this. She feels guilt, and other things I am too young to decipher. She'd hoped the separation had occurred when I was young enough to simply not remember. Easier that way, for everyone.

We sit in silence for a second, or for an age—time seems to lose its grip on the moment. The train is crossing the tracks at the far end of the property, a clanging, uneven song that announces the afternoon. I can't tell if I've done something wrong, if I've broken some rule I was unaware of. It's so hard to tell what's wrong from what isn't.

She hesitates. Her throat flutters as the words are formed carefully:

"It took more love for her to give you up than it would have to take you with her."

Her voice is deliberately soft, tremulous and careful. It saddens her to say it. The song of a wounded bird that sings to give itself comfort. As though a misuse of tone will fracture the unseen barrier protecting that place, keeping us content and together in our little world.

The words will be repeated many times throughout my early years, as if rehearsed, as if read from a prompt in her mind.

Her hand caresses my hair, the same color as her own, and she returns to the kitchen. The house stays silent for a time, and then her singing fills it again. The electric fan, though it never stopped running, resumes its whirring. The hummingbirds return to feed.

The volcanic mountain in the north has just erupted. The sky is still clear, but soon—in a day or maybe two—it will darken. Quiet black rain will fall, fine but everywhere, filling the air with a chemical firework smell and coating the world with ash, with a film of grayish grit that will last until the rain finally washes it away.

The Luckiest Kid

"Idyllic" is the word I typically use when describing my childhood. It would be the first thing I'd tell you if you asked. For all the unusual circumstances, I was very much loved. I was cared for and prided upon. No one abused me. No one forced me to do anything I didn't want to do. I didn't have to grow up before I was ready or consider anything outside of the bubble of tranquility I'd been deposited into. Quite the opposite, really. I was completely free, given leave to roam the roughly five hundred acres that my grandparents owned.

My days were equal parts active and serene. Dogs and cats and chickens and horses, sassy pygmy goats, wide marshes and hayfields, secret places hidden in briar patches, in tall grass. The dogs would dig shallow tunnels under barbed-wire fences to escape from the house's main yard into the fields beyond and I would follow them through, to places I wasn't supposed to go, until my grandmother would call me and I would come back, hands and knees crusted with new dirt. The oak trees were twisted from growing on a slope, leaving hollows in which only a small child would fit. I would hide there, oblivious to the sap that would adhere permanently to my clothes and have to be cut out of my hair. I was the only one small enough to fit. That had to mean something. The tree was inviting me to crawl in.

I loved my home. I loved the animals, the open spaces, the old barn, the fields of tall hay-grass through which I could tunnel or barrel.

I caught grasshoppers and spiders and lizards in jars with neighbor kids. I swam in the shallow river on the edge of our property. I waded the edges in search of tadpoles. I climbed and fell out of trees. I daydreamed endlessly, about the things just beyond the edge of reality, little fantasy worlds in which I was someone else, in which the inexplicable things I saw on television and in books were real.

It was a young boy's fairy tale—except in my own quiet moments when I was alone with my thoughts and the activities of the day had come to an end. The quiet was like a little song, accentuated by the chorus of frogs in the meadow pond to the side of the house, and by the seemingly constant breeze that whipped through the trees. Then, I felt a formless and remote but ever-present shadow over everything I knew. A knot in the grain. Then, in those moments, I felt abandoned and alone.

◦—◦ ⊫✦⊟ ◦—◦

We lived in a pale green ranch house that my grandfather and his extended family had built themselves in the early 1950s. It was decently spacious and fairly empty, just my grandparents and me and a houseful of trinkets and contraptions and art and books that seemed like they had all been deposited into the house from a parallel universe in which time moved slower, or perhaps altogether differently. In a way, they had. My grandparents had been born in the dying breaths of the depression; their parents had instilled in them a compulsion to save, to reuse, to repurpose everything that could be salvaged. The house was full of old and interesting things awaiting their new purpose, their new lease on life.

Other people came and went, family and other guests, but the core of the house was us three and the innumerable pets that my grandparents adored like their own offspring. There was always at least one cat and one dog, but more often there were multiples of each. One of them would die and be mourned like the lost member of the family that they truly were. Soon after, they would be replaced by another, but the dead would never be forgotten. My grandmother would always keep them alive in her exceptional memory, and her stories about King, the rock-eating dog; Sparks, the injured and domesticated owl who one day had had enough of humans and simply flew away; and Snowball, the three-legged cat with a heart of gold, were common occurrences at dinner and before bed. I loved hearing her talk about her beloved pets. Her voice always took on a tone of joy at the nostalgia that, in retrospect, her talk of the present did not.

6

My books and toys were strewn about the place, collected periodically with exasperation at my ability to destroy the house and then placed back in my bedroom for me to scatter again. I loved board games, but I usually didn't have anyone to play them with me unless I could convince my grandmother to stop her incessant housework and caring for things, so I'd usually just play them with myself. Half-finished games of Clue and chess and Monopoly and Risk were set up in odd places and left half-played, in case I wanted to go back after my attention had been diverted elsewhere to finish them, giving the impression that invisible players—ghosts, perhaps—engaged in board games in corners of rooms, on the unused end of the dining room table, where people only sat during family functions.

There were people who knew the circumstances of why I was there, living in that house without my parents. Some thought it a cruel thing that I had been dumped on aging grandparents who had already raised their children and should be enjoying the rewards of their years of hard work: the quiet, the calm, the easy slide into retirement by then. In a way, they were right, but I think my grandparents would have lost their minds had they nothing and no one to care for. It was all they knew how to do.

My grandfather was one of a batch of children born close together who'd all had to fend for themselves at a young age. He had been expected to work, to earn his way, to be a man when he was still a boy. He took to it well; he was a gentle bull of a man who loved his family without reserve and laughed openly and irreverently at most everything. But the early years of hard work and being cast out on his own too early had left their mark as well. Like a calf weaned too soon, he inherently needed mothering.

This would fall to his wife, someone with convenient years of experience. My grandmother had practically raised her younger siblings while her mother and father worked. They drank their nights away while she labored to care for children not her own. The scars of it still blazed bright in the worry she carried even when she smiled, in the wringing of her hands when anyone made themselves a cocktail or opened a bottle of wine.

That could be the one, I imagine her thinking, *the one that hooks you.*

Her emotional damage was broadcast outward and reflected in the healing she tried constantly to promote in everyone, in every living thing within range. She was an emotional missionary, and the world as she saw it was beset with untreated wounds. The dogs, the cattle, the cats, the chickens—they all seemed like family, and my grandmother mourned the inevitable loss of each one like they were. By the time I was ten years old, we had our own makeshift pet cemetery.

Even inanimate objects mattered.

"Poor little swing set," she said one morning as we returned to the house from feeding cows and chickens. I had been given a swing set for an early birthday, flimsy but functional with red-and-white candy cane stripes along the metal frame. The red paint had peeled and faded from years of rain, and rust had taken over. I had long outgrown it, and now it sat like a ruin in the backyard.

"Nobody loves it anymore."

I had loved it, but it seemed old to me now. And either way I could no longer sit in the tiny seat to swing myself, even if I'd wanted to.

Her pity, the bottomless well of sadness and love at the core of her, took hold. The swing set must be saved. In her mind it was lonely, forlorn at my absence. A few days later, she had my grandfather load it into the back of his work truck and take it away, to be loved by less fortunate children somewhere, I was told. I wonder now if that was just a lie to keep the peace, and the tired thing was simply disposed of. I also wonder if it was indeed given to other children who quickly outgrew it and now sits somewhere else, lonely and rusting, waiting for someone to love it again.

My grandparents were well matched in their need for healing. They fit better in ways that no one could see than in the ways that were visible to the outsider. My grandfather's booming voice and irreverent sense of humor filled the house when he was home, a fitting contrast to my grandmother's soft anxiety. He allowed whatever, whenever, as far as the house was concerned. His work, his shop, his outside daily activities—those were his areas of dominion. Indoors, his wife was the boss. He ruled at work, and at home I think it benefitted his mental state to not care about most things. He liked to cook dinner for everyone, and he liked reading western novels.

Their legacy—the legacy of their generation, it seems to me now—was their well-raised brood. The children must be put first. They must be given the things we never had. They must be protected from the pain of the world, from its hard edges. My grandmother's overabundant care led to spoiled children, a spoiled husband, spoiled pets, and spoiled livestock.

But by my time, her children had gone away, off into their own adulthoods. Her parents and siblings, the ones she had cared for like a mother, were gone, too. Her husband was a devoted and loving man, but absent in his own way, absorbed in multiple levels of work because work was all he knew. She was, but for me, alone in so many ways.

I was hers now, to care for, because no one else could do it so well. Raising a child in her forties and fifties couldn't have been easy, but she would have it no other way. A void was left with the growing of her children, and the passing of her parents, and somehow I filled it.

I was the cure for her loneliness, and the majority of her love would be focused on me. It was endless. I knew nothing else. But somewhere beneath the shine of those days, of the happiness that was projected through the place like the gleam of sun on polished glass, was a tarnished reputation, a black mark on some imaginary family crest that only she could see.

◦—◦ ▆◆▆ ◦—◦

Where were my mother and father?

I knew, and I didn't.

At first, I asked questions about my parents, like any young person would. They were answered with kindness and sincerity. Everyone had the same reply, or a variation of the original, which always came from my grandmother: My parents were too young. They mutually decided to separate, and after a series of cloudy events I landed in the only place available to me. The seat of the family.

How, exactly? Over and over I asked. I wanted to understand the *how* of it, the basic mechanics behind a mother leaving her child behind. I was too young to understand that not all mothers are alike. Every single one I knew carried their newborns around like hard-won trophies, like a badge that proved with tangible certainty their status as a woman. How could mine have simply handed me over and vanished?

There was a carefully maintained blind spot where my mother was concerned. My grandparents, my aunts and uncles, even my father—no one ever said anything bad about her. But neither did anyone ever really explain why she was gone.

She was spoken of tenderly, always with careful repetition, like an angel, or a martyr who had sacrificed herself—or me, depending on the rendition—for some greater good. She was "nervous," which I would later come to know actually meant "argumentative in a family that collectively fears and despises conflict on all levels." She started fights and my father avoided them. She was a troubled, fragile person, I was told, who'd been forced by unforeseen circumstances into leaving me behind for the betterment of everyone involved. She had asked for permission to leave me where she knew I'd be cared for. It took more love, I was told so many times, for her to give me up than it would have to take me with her into the ether of the world, to wherever she had gone.

It was the only story I was ever told, so I believed it. Everyone agreed: family, friends, everyone. Even my teachers at school had a variation of the story to repeat back to me when I talked about her to other students, or to those same students when they asked why my grandmother was always at my school functions but never my father or mother.

I was too young to see how much more there was to the story, but even in my earliest memories of having it explained to me it felt somehow off. The disparity between the things I was told and the love and absolute mothering I received constantly from my grandmother left a tangle of confusion in my mind, a convoluted mass of mixed emotions and questions I didn't know how to properly ask.

There was no anger in the things they told me. No one disparaged her. And yet this strange balance of information and the lack of it left me with the impression that she was somehow disliked, or that they feared her somehow.

⊷ ⇌✦⇋ ⊶

Riddle, Oregon, is a small town, just over a thousand people today, and that sense of seclusion still lingers there—a feeling of being at once both safe and trapped, either cut off or protected from reality, from the goings-on of the world outside. The interstate was only a few miles away, the great rushing vein of traffic by which to escape, though few did. Even when the abundance of work and money had faded completely and the town felt like a ruin in which scavengers and lonely ghosts still clung.

Industry was once the town's livelihood, its blood and muscle. Riddle quickly grew from a railroad stop and a post office into an actual community sometime in the early 1900s when the lumber mills and loggers first set up shop. There was also a sprawling nickel mine, built at the top of the nearest and tallest mountain, where a massive deposit of the metal was discovered and mined since the 1940s. Combined with the abundance of tree-related jobs, farms, and cattle ranches, it was a good place to earn a living for most of the century.

I was born at the end of the 1970s, during the final breaths of a long-lived economic era, the golden financial bubble in which small-town America had flourished since World War II. The end was definitely nigh, but not yet alarmingly visible. The timber industry was still going at close to full throttle. The sawmills and logging companies paid well and cared for their employees. One man working full time at the mills brought home a paycheck sufficient to keep his family thriving and happy. He could afford to buy and maintain a house, a plot of land, a sport vehicle for the weekends, everything that made for the good life. Disco was still a big thing, and *Star Wars*—the original *Star Wars* film, presaging the glorious advent of the cinematic space opera in the mainstream. In the coming decade, the genre would saturate the market on every level.

My parents were young when I was born: my father was barely nineteen, my mother a few months older. They were high school students in the same grade, the same school. My mother, a friend of my father's twin sister, became a household regular in the place, strangely, where I would spend my childhood without her.

Small towns have a strange way of matchmaking, even when there's little or no match to be found. Seemingly random people who can't stand each other just pair up and start reproducing, even when they're essentially still children and know next to nothing of themselves, or about the workings of the world they inhabit. Who knows anything of love and partnership at nineteen years old? At such a changeable age, is anyone really capable of making that kind of decision with certainty? Love is something different to a young mind: less enduring, less factual, more lust and hunger to be loved by anyone willing.

Or maybe that's the jaded fortysomething in me talking. Me, who didn't marry until the end of my thirties. Me, who feared commitment even as I committed to it.

What is certain is that my mother loved her husband's parents, her new family, and they loved her. All the various accounts I've ever heard on the matter line up on this one thing. The only son had found a wife. A grandchild was on the way. It was perfect. It was a reward for parenting done right, and my mother would be welcomed into the fold openly, joyously.

＊＋　▤＊▤　＋＊

My parents' general absence wasn't strange to me. I was too young to know otherwise. They had divorced before I was capable of remembering it. They were gone, and it was just how it was.

"But they love you very much," my grandmother told me endlessly. "It wasn't because of you." There was a note in her voice every time she said it, a specific tone. I can hear it now. To a four-year-old it was simply the sound of her, but it was pain. I understand that now.

My father was there sometimes, always briefly. This should have been of interest to me, that my father was sometimes present and sometimes it was like he had never existed in the first place, but it wasn't. Like any of the other peculiarities in that portion of my life, it was just *how it was*. He was in and out, visiting but never for long, a fleeting presence, but always seemingly happy to see me, sometimes carefree and sometimes stern, always just out of reach. It was his way. He would be around for a while and then gone again in an instant—or at least that's the lasting effect he has left in my memory.

He loved me. He still does, I know it, but I don't know if he ever wanted to be a parent. I don't know if he was very good at it. What teenager is? The world was different then, and he was expected to be a dutiful, committed parent at twenty years old. Why he chose to step away from it completely is one of many questions with no answer. Why he deferred to his own parents' judgment on the matter of, at the time, his only child is a mystery I say I've stopped trying to solve, but what child could? Maybe he was just too young. I know I would have been.

My grandmother was right, though. I knew he loved me. He said it frequently enough. But the distance of our relationship, especially in the years to come, would not lend much weight to those words. As far as I can understand, he is a man alone in the universe in his head. No one is in there with him. It's just how he is—naturally distant, with no clear intention behind it.

Am I like him? Every child asks something similar. *What would I be like if I had my own son? Would I be so distant? So willing to stay away?*

One of the earliest memories of him is also one of my fondest, without bias or the odd and confusing questions of later that made me sad or angry or distant in my own way. A handsome, dark-bearded man standing in denim overalls on the edge of the creek behind my grandparents' property, on the edge of the largest hayfield. He's holding a fishing pole and smoking either a joint or a cigarette, waiting for something to take the bait, while I swim upstream from the hook. He's laughing at me as I try to breaststroke in two feet of water, smoke erupting from his nostrils, from around whatever he's smoking that's held between his teeth.

I ask him if he's going to catch a shark, and he says, "I hope so, buddy. We'll have river shark for dinner." I laugh at the notion of my grandma cooking a whole shark in her kitchen—one of the great whites I'd seen on television, boat-sized and snapping angrily as she wrestled it into a tub-sized pot.

If my father was around but also absent, my mother was the opposite. Gone, but available. She was present in all the ways that my father, who lived so much closer, was not.

The circumstances of this arrangement were indeed confusing, and still are, in a way. I didn't question my father's emotional absence; I lacked the ability to. But my mother was a fixture, invisible and far away. I knew her. She called often enough, and I quickly came to associate the ringing of our bright orange rotary-dial telephone with her unseen presence, as though it was a sound that only she could make, a reminder of the extra invisible parent I had.

I can't recall our conversations now, but I do recall the sound of her voice. In those memories there is an undercurrent of sadness to her tone. Did I invent it? Was I capable of understanding it then?

She was never completely gone, but distance is distance to a child. The hands-on parenting was left to the only people who seemed capable of it—the ones who had become my parents in lieu of my own who were both missing in their own ways.

I was allowed to call my mother whenever I felt the need, but I was always slightly apprehensive. What if she didn't want to talk to me?

She sent letters and birthday gifts. I sent pictures of houses and castles drawn in purple crayon. She asked for more, and I took to creating a supply, in case she wanted them. The crayon said "blue-violet," but I called it purple. It seemed like the only color that made sense for the occasion.

I never asked her why she left me. I don't know why I didn't. Every child wonders if they did something wrong, I suppose, and for all of the adults telling me that it wasn't the case in my situation, I think I feared that response or something close to it. Something that would place the fault on me. For being born, perhaps, or for being a difficult child.

When she did visit, a rare occasion to a child's mind in which time is a sluggish, stubborn thing, the strain on every adult in the room was palpable. It was always an event for me, better than Christmas, better than my birthday, better than any other car that pulled into the driveway and set the dogs to barking. Every time, I had to relearn her face and the sound of her voice. I had to overwrite the memory from the visit before, the image that time had distorted. When she left, I would always long to go with her, and my emotional outbursts and general behavior would always be described as "terrible, just terrible" in the days following her departure.

What did they expect?

She was sarcastic, acerbic sometimes, and I emulated it as often as I could. I recall the faces of my aunts and grandparents when I did. Slight cringe. Near-imperceptible anxiousness at the tone, at the statement I had just made and probably didn't fully understand.

She was also pretty, much more so than the other mothers I knew. Light hair when everyone's in my household was dark. Bright green eyes where everyone's in my father's family were brown. My own eyes were equal parts of both colors, and I longed for them to turn completely green someday. She was less matronly, and thinner. Her hair was styled better, in more of a modern way. She walked and talked with a fire behind her that the adult women in my life lacked, like they were afraid of the world and she wasn't.

I prided myself somehow on having such a beautiful smart-ass for a mother, even if she was in many ways not my mother and had left me to be raised by other less flashy, less amazing people, no matter how much they loved me.

I would come to feel shame for this, though I can't recall if I came to feel it on my own, or if it was instilled. How dare I want for anything else? How dare I ever feel ungrateful to the people who'd given me everything? I was lucky.

⊷ ▰◆▰ ⊶

I *was* lucky. That's a fact, knowing what I do now. I was also told, over and over, that I was lucky. Every tantrum thrown, every scrap of anger or protest at anything that troubled my little existence, was met inevitably with a well-rehearsed proclamation of how fortunate I was. It was usually my grandmother, but others would chime in as needed, often with less kindness in their voices.

"What do you have to complain about?" my aunt Gail once demanded as I raged at being made to come inside during a thunderstorm. It seemed unfair that she was allowed to stay outside while lightning struck the fields and I wasn't. "Nothing, that's what," she snarled through her cigarette, through the wide front window that separated us. "You're the luckiest kid in the world and you don't care. You don't appreciate anything."

Gail was my father's older sister, the one who'd stayed close to home. She and my father's other sister honed their mothering skills on me before they had children of their own. They were harder on me than my grandmother ever would be, but even with them I didn't have to try very hard to get whatever I wanted. Point, grunt, whine, insist. Most requests

14

were granted with expedience, if only to quiet me. I was spoiled to the point of ridiculous, and Gail was one of the very few who would dare to challenge me. She was often a stern voice where my grandmother's was soft, and she understood things that my grandparents couldn't.

She fought with me like an older sister might have. We were evenly matched in our terrible moods, and my father commented several times on the similarities between us in terms of our sour, shitty attitudes on a bad day. I heard her referred to as "homely" when I was very young, and felt a stab of sadness and anger on her behalf when I learned years later what it meant. I thought, like all young children do with their parent figures, that she was pretty.

It was Gail who gave me my first cigarette. She swore me to secrecy as she handed me the pack: Camel 99s, only two left in the box.

"Now, listen." She pointed a squarish French-tipped fingernail at my face. "Mom will lose her fucking mind if she finds out, and she'll blame me. So only smoke behind the woodshed."

I always did, but my grandmother still eventually found out, and the look of heartbreak on her face is still burned into me. She hated cigarettes, my grandmother. Her mother had died when I was very young, of emphysema, from a long lifetime of cigarette smoking. A terrible thing, to watch someone you love slowly choke to death. The trauma of that event was visible in her. That all of her children grew up to be smokers must have felt like a failure on her part. Every drag of a cigarette I've taken since the day she caught me has been tinged with guilt.

My only recollections of my great-grandmother are her hair, still coal black in her eighties, and her hands, withered and covered in blue veins from age and wasting. I remember my great-grandfather a bit more clearly. He seemed a miserable man to me. He had been a drinker, an *alcoholic*—a word my grandmother always said in a hushed tone, like the shame of it was infectious. I assume now that the hushed tone was a placeholder for other words, among them *abusive* or worse. He bemoaned the death of his wife loudly, like he expected someone to do something about it, like his own family was indebted to him for the loss. He treated me well, but his harsh, expectant tone with the rest of the world, and especially with my grandmother—his own daughter and my acting mother—made me afraid of him and resentful of his presence. He whined loudly and bemoaned his loneliness to her like she'd had some part in it. Like she didn't miss her dead mother just as much as he missed his dead wife.

When I came home from school one day and he had died too, I expected the same sadness from my grandmother that she had exhibited whenever she spoke of her mother, but instead she came to me and smiled as I stepped off the school bus. The house was full of relatives, but she just smiled and held me in the front yard while they watched from the living room windows.

⊷⊷ ⊯⊹⊵ ⊷⊷

I was a young tyrant in the house, but I was also generally adored for being a funny and intelligent child. Having learned to talk to adults before I learned to talk to other children allowed me to cast a valuable illusion of smarts I didn't really have. I did not excel at most subjects in school. In fact, I hated most of them, and generally refused to even try if things were too immediately difficult. But my charm, and the speaking tricks I'd learned from everyone around me, made me a welcome addition to most conversations, and I loved conversing.

The household was something of an ensemble cast. Some relative or other was always staying with us temporarily, an aunt or a cousin. People visited frequently—neighbors and relations and the odd old family friends in RVs and camper trailers towed on oversized trucks. It made for interesting, diverse interactions. I delighted in entertaining guests, as did my grandmother. She was more bored with her life than I realized at the time. Guests were a welcomed distraction.

There was always someone pulling into the driveway, unannounced and uninvited, to visit or to ask a favor. They would be welcomed in warmly, regardless of the day's requirements. Everything would stop. Coffee would be brewed. The table would be hastily set (my job, frequently, and I was good at it). Whatever was so important before the dogs announced a guest, it could wait until after lunch.

So strange, that inclination to just show up at someone else's home without informing them first. So old-fashioned. If someone rings my doorbell without messaging me first, I hit the floor like it's a fucking air raid. I climb up on the kitchen counter to peer down at the stoop, anxious, since it's probably a serial killer come to collect my skin or my organs, or possibly someone with a clipboard and a heart full of golden good intent (and a not-so-clever donation pitch). Either way, no one's home.

But not in the house I grew up in. All were welcome, even on bad days. Even in the worst of weather, with the worst of life circumstances hanging overhead.

Relatives were always within reach, just across the fence, within shouting distance. Everyone had their own lives, their own jobs and spaces and activities that involved being gone, but our house was the hub. It was a focal point of activity, though it was in the middle of nowhere, eight miles outside of Riddle, the nearest town. Perhaps for its size, or because it was naturally the most active of the available homes, every holiday function, every family-based event, took place in our dining room, our backyard where extra chairs and tables would be set out for the deluge of guests we hadn't anticipated.

Friends of the family made use of the property too. When the son of a former neighbor, a childhood friend of my father's, put a gun to his head in a moment of despair and pulled the trigger, the family, naturally heartbroken, was invited by my grandparents to hold his memorial at their house. They had no real stake in the man's death, or his life, as he had moved away, across the country to Florida many years prior. It was simply, to them, the only thing that made sense. Gathering, nurturing, holding on—it was what they knew, what they were good at. Tragedy on that scale could only be addressed by bringing it home.

Most of the relatives and neighbors and friends who visited were much older, in their fifties and above, far past the age of giving a damn about most things. Their humor has definitely shaped me, and their wisdom, however outdated it might be now. My grandfather's older sisters were particularly hilarious. They had a slightly sinister, slightly perverse style of amusement at the world and its infinite stupidity. They seemed like royalty to me when they visited, like specially privileged aristocrats. The aunts were allowed to smoke in the house. They always did it the same: in a far-off corner of the dining room beneath an open window, a blue crystal ashtray—the only one in the house that I can recall, that only they ever made use of—in their free hand. Their long red fingernails and oversized earrings would gleam like polished gems in the afternoon sun.

They laughed at my jokes, and praised my drawings and discoveries. Aunt Peggy shrieked and squirmed, gleefully, as I paged through picture books filled with images of snakes and scorpions and tarantulas she would never see in real life. Aunt May said words that my grandmother and her friends avoided and abhorred, and openly talked shit about people in a house where "if you can't say something nice…" was the law of the land. Her profanity was delightful.

"Fuck 'em if they can't take a joke."

She said it to my grandfather over the Thanksgiving dinner table.

She was the oldest sibling, he the youngest. He never questioned her on anything, not even swearing at the dinner table, though I suspect that my grandmother would have preferred that he had.

The context of the statement is lost; I wasn't paying attention until she said it. But I remember thinking that it was the most brilliant, most artfully rude phrase in the English language despite the wide-eyed, silent scorn of my grandmother at the end of the table, spoonful of yams frozen in mid-serve until she corrected her expression and continued on with her matronly, understated control of the situation like Aunt May's words had never befouled her dining room.

That makes my grandmother sound stuffy and lacking in humor. She was neither of those things. She had a number of what she would call "off-color" jokes that she reserved for specific company (and certainly *not* the Thanksgiving dinner table). Specific company usually consisted only of her husband and her best friend, Donna, who lived about a mile away and visited frequently. The first of these jokes to come to mind was a little tale of a bouncing dildo that had gotten loose, somehow, and the women attempting to catch it—all of them in skirts, apparently. She could only refer to the thing as "you know, a *toy*," and she found the whole thing funnier than any one of her listeners. Her humor was definitely there. That's the point. But she only made use of it on specific occasions, in specific company. Her husband's sisters were too loud, too "bawdy old girl" in general to understand how funny my grandmother could be. I think it resulted in a quiet lack of respect on their part. Whenever they visited, my grandmother seemed less like the lady of the house and more like paid help with nothing to contribute to any conversation taking place.

She was prudish, though, which gave the immediate impression that she was thin-skinned and perhaps boring, when in fact she was sensitive to heightened emotion and especially to vulgarity. It bothered her when people swore or shouted, but she did it herself sometimes (though never to the level of the people around her, including her husband and his raucous sisters). I imagine her particular sensitivities were a by-product of her harsh upbringing, but she never spoke of that too much, except to say that there were issues with her father, and that her parents drank too much. I suspect that there was much more to the story, and that, as the oldest child in the family, she bore the brunt of her father's alcoholism and verbally abusive nature.

In truth, she was hysterically funny sometimes. I don't know how many people ever saw that side of her outside of the household. Both of my grandparents were. They delighted in embarrassing me with spontaneous, impromptu "old people dancing" as I called it, or with an inappropriate joke whispered from one to the other in public that made them both blush and then cackle at my horror. My grandmother especially enjoyed a good practical joke, scaring my grandfather when she could by jumping out of darkened closets and from around hallway corners with hands formed into tiny claws, or covering herself with a blanket and lying flat on the floor only to pop up when he entered the bedroom. He would often be visibly annoyed, which only made her breathless laughter ring through the house louder.

◄── ◄█◆☰ ──►

I never knew what to call the place. Some members of my family called it "the farm," but in the second grade my teacher, Mrs. Priem, corrected me when I told her about the cows that dominated most of the property. In all of my memories of the woman, she seems to be a hundred feet tall with hair made of wrought iron.

"Farm is plants and chickens. But *ranch*…" She drew out the word for my benefit, like it was the first time I'd heard it. "Ranch is big animals. Cows and horses. Understand?"

I didn't mention the orchard.

The orchard—pears and apples, and the oldest part of the property— was something of a mystery in the family. It seemed like each person in the house had their own version of its origin. My grandfather said it was planted by his relatives when they'd first arrived from Virginia in the 1920s. My grandmother told me it was already there, planted meticulously in four neat rows by persons unknown. My father said his parents had planted it, but neither of them took credit.

My great-aunt Peggy—my grandfather's beehive-sporting, chain-smoking, perpetually wisecracking older sister—said that the pink pear and apple trees "just grew like that," in four almost-perfect rows, as though they were asking to be fenced in squarely to prevent the cows and horses from getting accidentally drunk on their fermented late-spring fruit, grown heavy and fallen to the ground for the sun to turn to wine-smelling pulp that the livestock would rush to lick up with their disturbingly long tongues. They could fall, I was told, and be unable to get up for being so intoxicated—a fatal condition for a rotund thousand-pound grazing beast. Like an ocean cephalopod run ashore, the weight of their own bodies would slowly crush their insides.

"NO pears, Bluebell!"

19

My grandmother would shout it from the kitchen window that faced the orchard to the back of the house.

Bluebell was a spoiled cow whose mother had died birthing her. Like every creature on that ranch, myself included, she had been hand-reared with an excess of care by my grandmother, who was only capable of loving too much. Now fully grown, Bluebell had no fear of humans, and no respect whatsoever for the flimsy-looking fence that separated her from enjoying happy hour in the warm shade of pear trees along the line of square wire that separated pasture from orchard. Her black tongue would flail in the grass for rotting pears, nose jutting comically between the rectangles of rusted wire that bent like straw from the force of her.

"You'll get in trouble if you eat those pears, damn you!" And she'd tear out the back door, hurriedly kicking off her house slippers and stuffing her feet into rubber boots left on the porch for specifically the occurrence. Then, down the muddy path to the orchard, dogs at foot, to shoo another of her strays from certain doom, the screen door slamming loudly behind her and disrupting, briefly, the tranquility that settled over the house on most afternoons.

Afternoons were always my favorite. I hated school, but those lovely hours after the school bus deposited me at the bumpy gravel driveway were the best: quiet, but with enough background activity to remind me that I wasn't alone. The afternoon sun would filter in through the large stained-glass owl hanging in the front room, and through the aging yellow glass of the French doors that connected the house to the dining room. This was a touch my grandmother had insisted upon when they'd built the place, a little love song to the southern French revival architecture she adored, though she never called it by that name. On my eighth birthday, during one of the countless fights I had with one of my cousins, I accidentally tore one of the French doors off its hinges. It was repaired soon after, with no visible damage to be seen, but my grandmother looked at me that day like I'd shot one of the dogs.

What I remember most, and with the purest fondness of all of my childhood memories, are the days when I didn't have school, and no one was there but me, my grandmother, the dogs, and cats. They are often the coldest and foggiest days in my memories, but the morning mist and the damp bite in the outside air are comforting to me, a contrast to the warmth of the house and to the happiness of remembering those times.

We had our own world, and our own daily routine. My grandfather woke and left for work early—far earlier than anyone should have to. If I was lucky, I'd wake in time to help prepare his lunch and send him off, but I have never been a naturally early riser, so this was a rarity.

Then it was just the two of us, and the animals of the ranch in need of tending. It was my grandmother's pleasure and self-appointed responsibility to do so. She could have hired help to do it. She could probably have asked a nearby family member. But she loved it, and so did I by way of her joy at the task. We would—me, her, and three large and poorly behaved dogs—pile into the old truck that only remained for the singular purpose of feeding livestock, and drive to the old barn that was built so long ago that my grandfather couldn't recall the exact year of its construction. We would lift the heavy bales of hay into the truck, together, as some of them were so heavy that it took both of us, and drive down to the fields or the little hill where the cattle were kept. They knew us, knew it was time for breakfast, and would follow the slow-moving truck, mooing loudly as my grandmother drove along with the radio playing as I threw flat squares of hay from the back of the truck. The dogs would follow on foot, happy as any living creatures, keeping their distance from the hoofs and tempers of the cows, who had no tolerance for the dogs and their shenanigans, especially around their calves.

The entire scene is perpetually shrouded in morning mist in my recollection. It couldn't have always been there, given that this routine occurred throughout the year, but it comforts me, somehow, the early morning-ness of it, the glittering reflection of sunlight on the grass. I doubt I cared at all in the moment, but it adds something to the fondness of it that I'm glad to have taken with me.

With cows contented, we'd go home and make breakfast for ourselves. My grandmother would help me with my homework, and then I'd go do whatever I did afterward that I can't recall now. It was a strange ritual, looking back. I can't remember if I loved it then, but I do in retrospect. It was preferable to school, anyway, and I recall being at school in those days, wishing it was a Saturday so I could be with my grandmother and the dogs and cows instead of trapped in a room with other kids I didn't like, learning things I didn't want to learn.

My grandfather would come home from work in the afternoon, and the scene would change again. His boisterous energy would recast the house in a different light. He was always happy to see me and my grandmother. He'd flirt with her in the kitchen, winking at me when he knew he'd gone just a bit too far and was in danger of admonishment, a frequent thing.

My grandfather, like his sisters, was able to laugh at anything. It was a trait that could lighten the mood of the entire house if he needed it to. He was remote, in the way of the working man, but there was no doubt in anyone's mind that he loved his children and grandchildren more than anything else. It was apparent in the way he gently teased us and encouraged our weird respective quirks. He was a gentle soul who'd been toughened by a life of working tirelessly to provide, but he never lost his impish, ironic spark, not even on his deathbed.

They'd plan dinner—another ritual, even if we had no guests that evening. I loved helping, which they knew, and I'd be given a set of kitchen tasks to complete. Again, far preferable to schoolwork or most anything else. If we had guests, it became a more elaborate thing. Special dinnerware might be taken from the special shelves in the dining room cabinet that I was not allowed to go near. Spices and herbs that never left the rack might be searched out for use—pungent sage and earthy white pepper. They were things we never made use of in our own daily meals, but my grandmother always knew of regional and ethnic dishes that they might be used for. It was a game that I loved, asking her what marjoram was for, or curry powder, or star anise. She could have made up fake dishes for all I know now, but I don't care and I certainly didn't then.

⊷ ⊷ ⊷ ⊷

It was almost perfect, an almost perfectly happy early life. But something was missing, something that caused me a vague early form of pain—at once sharper for being so unfamiliar, yet dulled somewhat by the lack of understanding. That much I knew, though over time I stopped reminding myself. It hardened into the structure of me. I became a sad kid. An angry kid. The younger children in my family lived in fear of my rages, which were unpredictable and profound. I was mouthy and disobedient. I swore like an adult under my breath. I lied and played tricks with no conscience about it, no guilt at all, though being caught in a lie was one of the few things that would result in actual punishment.

When I was six, my father remarried, and by the time I was ten he'd had two other sons with his second wife. I was happy to have brothers, even if they felt like cousins—removed, visiting on holidays or when my father brought them. His attention toward me would be reduced by his second marriage and younger children before I was old enough to resent. I suppose that's a blessing, really. I never felt anger toward my brothers for being born. My father was just distant. I was cared for by better parents anyway, I told myself.

He grew ever more unavailable as I grew older, and his second wife did not get on well with my grandparents and aunts, who were always

22

around. I imagine this made it difficult to arrange any kind of regular visits. He would appear briefly, and then be spirited back to his other life by familial commitments and work and perhaps a general unease of playing the role of parent to the child he'd basically signed over any right to.

I must have mentioned it to my grandmother at some point, this noticeable remoteness. It hurt her, angered her, I recall from the scalded look on her normally serene face, to hear it come out of my mouth. Not long after I overheard her admonishing my father for ignoring me.

"I know, Mom. I'm sorry. I've been really busy."

"He doesn't understand that and you know it."

Her tone with him was soft, drifting out of the kitchen and into the adjacent dining room where no one knew I listened, but underneath it was a current of scorn. We lived in a very small town. Divorce was still an unusual thing. My grandmother abhorred the notion, and I think it shamed her that her own son had stained his name (and her own) by agreeing to one—then after it was done, it wounded her deeper than she knew to think that her own child was somehow unwilling or incapable of taking responsibility for *his* own child. To compensate, and to erase what damage she could, she had taken it upon herself to do the child-rearing, and for all I grew to represent and mean to her and to my grandfather, there was still an air of failure that lingered, and a sense of resentment, both within and from outside of the family circle.

"I'll come down soon and take him for a day or two, once the boys aren't sick."

Once the boys aren't sick. Once work calms down. Once the weather improves.

Our interactions were always pleasant, but by the time I was in double digits his fatherly behavior was limited to an occasional scolding when I was out of line—usually due to my mouth and increasingly surly attitude as I grew older. I didn't resent him or his strange absence, but neither did I take him seriously or respect whatever authority he might try to exert over me. I didn't know how. He was simply too distant to take seriously.

When my mother remarried and had other children—two more sons, strangely, just like my father—I wondered if she'd finally decided that she wanted children. I wondered if she'd come back for me. Half of me hoped for it, though I couldn't say why. The other half of me feared it, and somehow knew what it would cost everyone involved.

It was a strange coincidence to me that both of my parents had remarried after my birth and had two more sons apiece with their second spouses. No one around me seemed to see how odd it was. They were both present and seemingly capable parents for their newer children. I didn't resent it, but I wondered what it might be like for my brothers never to have experienced the vague sense of displacement and wordless longing I had. Even in my earliest memories, I have no recollection of my parents' marriage or its end, but my entire life has been spent in the wake of that end.

Missing someone you can't entirely remember is confusing to a child. It fucked with my mood more than I was capable of understanding. I was more and more angry as I grew up. I sometimes wonder if it affected my ability to comprehend the world around me, too; I was always a bad student. I was obedient enough and seemingly intelligent, but I never had any interest in learning and it showed early on. It baffled more than a few teachers, I'm sure. I seemed quite capable, could carry on a conversation at an adult level, and could read books several "levels" above my grade, but my grades never reflected any particular aptitude or brightness on my part. School was a burden and I just wanted to stay home.

Did it have something to do with my parental situation? So many kids had it so much worse than me, and a number of them were top students, athletes in the making, models of pending adulthood. I was not. I generally lagged behind, and I didn't care that I lagged behind.

I missed something I'd never had. I knew that the woman who'd actually brought me into the world was out there in it, living a life without me. It felt like an invisible barrier had been erected that changed the rules of mother and child to keep us apart, which was truer than I could have known at the time. It made me feel jealousy for things I didn't understand, too, even though my life on the ranch was good and I was loved more than many kids ever are. It shamed me, made me feel ungrateful for the grandparents who'd been so kind to take me in when apparently no one else wanted me.

I stopped crying about my mother when I turned eleven. It still made me sad, but the quiet moments grew more bearable. The longing stopped making its way to the surface and overwhelming me to the point of spontaneous tears that I'd spent years learning to hide—sometimes at school, which was humiliating. The lost mother/absent father story grew tiresome. I disliked talking about it, but it seemed perpetually present, staring back at me in the faces of every intact mother-father-child unit I saw. It just didn't seem to matter anymore. I had parents, grandparents, stepparents, an abundance of relatives who adored me. It was too much work to dive back into the *whys* and *what-ifs* of it all. So many other children had it so much worse. They starved. They were beaten. They died in their sleep as their homes were bombed from the sky. The questions around why my mother never came back for me remained, but I ignored them.

—+ ᴇ◆ᴇ +—

My father's second marriage collapsed when I was in the seventh grade, and his behavior toward my younger brothers became markedly similar to how he had seemingly forgotten me. It was too late to feel any pain on my own behalf over it, but I felt sadness for my half brothers. My grandmother had, by this time, stopped expecting and pushing him to be a better, more involved parent.

I made do without a traditional father. I'm not special there. Many people make do with no one, and my father was never unkind. Our relationship was never bad, but it was never very good, either. I don't think he ever wanted to be a parent, though he never bore me ill will, as some unwilling parents do. Despite his lack of fatherly instinct, his seeming lack of interest in being present, I eventually decided that he had tried his best, given the odd circumstances, given how young he and my mother had both been when I was born. He wasn't malicious, just not great "dad" material.

—+ ᴇ◆ᴇ +—

"He's less innocent than you might think," my mother said. That began the conversation that changed my entire view of my childhood, of everything I've written before this paragraph. And then she paused. She hesitated, for fear of *something.*

We were talking on the phone. I was thirty-seven. We were talking, as we often did, about my father and his family, rehashing events and personalities and the motivations of each person involved—our secret healing ritual. Remembering and reevaluating the situation, no matter how many times it had been done already, somehow seemed to soothe wounds that might otherwise have festered or bled us dry.

My mother and I had become much closer as adults than we'd been as distant parent and confused child. Our relationship started to change for the better when I was in college. I think she knew she could be more honest with me after I'd left the nest because it would no longer look like she was trying to ruin my relationship with my father and his family if

25

she told me her side of things—namely, why I had been raised by them and not her.

She was different in so many ways from the people who'd raised me, and I was more like her than anyone realized at the time, including me. Looking back, I think that my father's family saw that. I think it unnerved them to hear my mother's long-absent tone echoed in the son she'd left behind. Genetics, possibly, or me patterning myself after someone I admired, but having her there, if only on the phone, if only at a distance, suggested that maybe there was another life for me, outside of the loneliness and suffocating conformity of "country life" and the small-town misery that I had grown to despise by the time I was in middle school. Over the years she had become someone I could speak plainly to on matters I would otherwise have had no one to talk with.

She was the first person I came out to, because she had been the only person I knew who had expressed her support of gay men and lesbians. My father's family masked their revulsion with pity and religion. Any talk of "the gays" would be swiftly avoided, the conversation rerouted to something more innocuous. Any talk of me being gay—a rarity, though it happened a few times—would be dismissed as nonsense by my grandmother. She wouldn't hear of it. Every standard parental excuse would be offered: just an awkward phase, raised around an excess of women, trauma from my parents divorcing (which I have exactly zero memories of), etc. But my mom didn't care. She wasn't surprised when I told her. It was a gift, that lack of concern. It allowed me to not care as much either, and to process my sexuality on my own terms.

I spoke with her that evening about resentments left over from my childhood, how my grandparents had never pushed me to work hard or strive for anything great. I talked about the fact that I'd had to learn everything about being an adult on my own. Everything a young person should know by the time they leave home, from laundry to paying bills, I didn't—and it had led to a number of terrible, easily avoided mishaps and small-scale disasters in my early twenties. I felt stunted by my lack of life skills, perpetually behind the curve.

I told her that I felt like I had no real place, like I was a child of two or more worlds but, because of the parental gray area in which I matured, I belonged to none of them.

She listened, as she always did. I was just venting. By my thirty-seventh year, my life had been decidedly rough in many places and disappointing in others—as lives are prone to be. I was recovering from a failed relationship. I'd been wounded by it. I was lonely. My self-imposed solitude was a fertile bed for unhappy thoughts. I was drinking wine, I recall, so I might have gone too far with my lamenting. I was just clearing out my own brain that night. I didn't expect my unhappiness to unearth a hidden trove of things I'd never been told. The conversation turned at some point to my father. What I thought I knew turned out to be only one side of things, an abridged version of why my mother had left me.

She's a well-spoken woman, my mother. She doesn't pause to find words, but she did that night. They were forming faster than she could speak them, a trait I've inherited. The pause meant something. A change had taken place in our dialogue. I could hear it over the phone: some invisible, inaudible twist in the tone of the conversation.

She would tell me, several years after this conversation, that she didn't know why she waited to tell me the truth of it all. She didn't know why she had allowed me to believe things about myself, my father, his parents, and her that weren't entirely (or completely) true. She said, simply, that she could no longer allow the lie to continue.

The lie. It hurt me to hear it described that way. It still does, as I write it now.

They had married and divorced young, that much is true. What changed is the details of afterward. What changed is the "why" in the question I'd asked of myself and everyone around me for my entire life: Why did my mother leave?

She didn't offer me up, like I was told.

I'm disinclined to think that anyone involved had malicious intent, not even my father. Everything about my childhood says the opposite. Everything I see in relation to my own upbringing, no matter how fucked up, ultimately appears to have been done with my best interest in mind. I can't see how anything other than love could have motivated my grandparents to behave the way they did in the wake of my parents' divorce. It must have felt like a failure for them, too. Perhaps more so than for my parents, to see their only son lose his wife. It must have frightened them to watch it occur, this dreaded thing they'd never had to do and would never consider for themselves. I can only assume they were trying to protect me from it in any way they could.

My mother was careful to point out that my grandparents weren't bad people—not at all and quite the opposite. She stressed the point before continuing. She wanted me to know that she never stopped loving them, even after losing me.

I can't say that any one person in the situation is to blame. Maybe that's the kid in me talking; at the end of the day we all just want our parents to approve of us, to love us with all of our flaws and fuckups. Maybe that's why, after hearing my mother's long-hidden side of the story, I still can't point the finger at anyone. They did what they did because they were trying to spare me from what they viewed as unnecessary sadness. And they succeeded, in a way.

My mother's version of events, the only concise and detailed version I've ever been given, went as follows:

When her marriage went bad, her own family was unwilling to help her. The "why" of their unwillingness is its own collection of disturbing and sad stories. My mother's parents were even younger than she and my father were when they started having kids—four of them, starting with her. Her mother was fifteen, her father barely seventeen when she was born. I shouldn't generalize too much, but it makes sense to me, at least, that they were fairly terrible parents.

My mother's mother was reserved. That's the best word I can use to describe her. She was a kindly enough, if distant, "grandparent" to me in the rare times when I saw her. At least, she was never unkind to me—but she was not a good mother. Her list of crimes and cruelties against her own children is extensive. By every account I've ever heard, she loved her children when they were convenient. When they were of use to her. And when they weren't, they were a nuisance and a burden—starting with the oldest child, my mother.

Her father was no better. He also refused to take his daughter in, to help her with her own child. I recall him being somewhat more "grandfatherly" to me. Even after my mother had left, he would visit on occasion, when I was very young, and I didn't mind him. But by the time I was eight his visits stopped and I had largely forgotten him as well. A few years later I was in a supermarket shopping with my grandmother when we encountered him. He greeted us warmly enough, though my grandmother had to remind me who he was: the other grandpa. He pushed an old, frail-looking woman in front of him in a wheelchair. She smiled at me. I was shy, so I said nothing beyond the "hello" expected of me.

"Getting big!" she laughed at my grandmother.

"Sixth grade next year."

"Well, bring him by sometime." Like it was overdue.

Hesitation. Awkwardness. A hurried goodbye with promises of a visit, which unnerved me. In the car, safely removed from these almost-strangers, my grandmother would tell me that the woman in the wheelchair was my great-grandmother. I had a vague memory of her from some meeting in the past, but it didn't match up with the ill-looking woman in the wheelchair.

Some people are just cruel. Some are just distant. Some feel too much, love too freely, give away their power. Blame nature or nurture or nothing at all—some people just aren't great parents, and some are. I've always wondered which I'd be, though I've never had any desire to have children of my own.

The important thing is: my mother's parents didn't care that she was out of options. She had been on her own for years already by the time she met my father, and when their marriage fell apart, she had no one to turn to except for his family. Where else could I have gone? She knew that taking me would expose us both to further hardship. She needed a job, income, a home for both of us. She was willing to make those things happen, but she needed to get on her feet after leaving my father, so she left me with him and his parents in what was supposed to be a temporary living arrangement. She would figure out the life stuff, the means by which to make it on her own with her son. Then she'd come back for me.

What changed after this is still a mystery, at least in terms of the motivation behind it. Again, I hesitate to call it malicious. But it's hard for me to say; I was a baby when it all took place. I have no memory of these events. I have no recollection of my parents being anything more than relative strangers whose only link is me, so it's hard to understand what happened next.

I imagine it's hard for my mother, too, to comprehend why, on attempting to collect me, she was served with a restraining order that prevented her from setting foot in the place that would become my childhood home, and from coming back for me as she had planned.

No one in my family had ever given me that piece of the puzzle. No one had ever alluded to it in any way. She had left me of her own volition, by every account I'd heard.

A custody battle was to ensue, but it would be short-lived. I had always been told that my mother missed her court date, but I would learn later from her, her sister, her cousins, from everyone who was there at the time and was not related to my father, that she had shown up and had been turned away under the false pretense that she wasn't allowed to take part without a lawyer of her own. My father told her this, standing there with his lawyer.

She was young. She believed him. Her lack of support and resources and my father's sudden increase in them would quash any hopes of a fair hearing on the matter. Legal representation is not cheap, and how a twenty-one-year-old man with no job came by his is another question that lingers, almost four decades later. I can only assume that my grandparents paid for it, that they acted out of a sense of fear over my fate, out of love for me. Anything else, any other avenue of thought, is too painful to imagine.

Did he look her in the eye when she learned that she'd lost her only child? Could he do it? Was he acting alone? Or were his parents, who gave me years and years of love and happiness, a part of the scenario as well? And my mother, was she devastated? Was it easy after the blow was struck? Did she miss me as much after her other children were born? Why did he lie so grievously, so permanently, and then leave me too?

There I stayed, for so long, in the lonesome comfort of the country, on the orchard/ranch/farm, loved, doted on, spoiled. But it was never enough. Something was missing, and at thirty-seven years old I fully understood what it was. They must have hoped that I would be too young to feel anything for the woman who'd only been there a short time. Easier for me, easier in general, and the least painful outcome, which I believe has always been the point of this mess.

⚬⟜ ⚞✦⚟ ⟞⚬

It occurs to me to question why I would blindly believe my mother's version of events, my absent mother, over the rest of my family. It wasn't exactly a contradiction—it was more of an addition, an addendum—but it's important for me to question it. So much was omitted. It seems like a required thing for me to weigh out every side of a story, every visible outcome in a narrative.

I believe her. I believe because she is the only one to offer anything in the way of details as to why things turned out the way they did. My grandparents, my father, my aunts and uncles and cousins from that side of my family, they all avoided talk of my living arrangements if they could, avoided any conversation involving my mother. They always waited for me to make my own conclusion. They said I was lucky, I was loved, I was wanted.

They were right, and yet something was still missing.

My mother also waited, and kept this information to herself, went along with what I believed to be true for more than thirty years. She waited because she knew the information would hurt me and would also have hurt my relationship with my grandparents. She knew that, in a way, it would poison me.

She waited until I was an adult to tell me these things, when maintaining a falsehood seemed tiresome and, finally, pointless.

"I didn't want to damage you in the process of defending myself," she told me.

Had she wanted to use me as a weapon against my family, she would have done so when I was young. She would have told me these things on the telephone during one of the many calls, in hopes that I would repeat them to my household. She wouldn't have waited until I had already flown the coop and had come to conclusions of my own. She wouldn't have suffered silently as I repeated falsehoods and abridged versions of events to her that she knew to be untrue, that she knew to be only a small piece of the story.

It took a long time, many months after the fateful conversation, for me to come to terms with it all. The change came slowly, despite how quickly the revelations were dropped in my lap. I was angry, of course. Furious. Then I felt guilt, though it seemed stupid to do so. I felt like I should have deduced the things my mother told me for myself, without having her there to explain them in detail. How could I have? Why did I feel responsible?

I considered confronting my father, my grandmother, anyone involved with the lie I'd been told. I never did, because I didn't believe I would get any answer that would matter. I had asked for answers from my father's family all through my life, and I never got them. Why would that change now, nearly four decades after the event? Why would they suddenly be able to give me their side of things when no one had been capable or willing when I lived there?

I settled on sadness. Sadness for my mother more than for myself. It pains me to think of how hard it must have been for her to see me grow up at a distance, especially with me never truly knowing why that distance existed between us. It makes me wish I could have done something to change it, to blot out the sad parts for both of us. But I feel freer for knowing the truth of my early years. In a way, the knowing broke an invisible chain that was holding me to that past version of myself, an old skin in need of casting off. I can still look back and feel happy that boy was given a good start and so much love, even if he is gone now. I had to leave, like my mother did. I never could go back. A strange repetition, but perhaps inevitable, given all that transpired and all that I am.

What kind of life would we have had, my mother and I, had I gone with her all those years ago? Another question I'll ask for the rest of my life, as I'm sure my mother will. It would have been hard, I suppose. I would probably be a vastly different person than I am now. Or maybe not. Maybe we're all fixed in place as soon as we're thrust into the world.

Did they feel guilt over it all? The details my mother gave were never once mentioned by them. According to what I knew as fact for most of my life, she was never forced out, and I was never intended to go with her. My grandmother's version varied somewhat: according to her I'd been given up out of desperation, by a damaged girl who didn't yet know how to be a mother, or if she wanted to be. Was that what she believed?

And my father—why would he go to such lengths, only to fade from parental view so soon afterward? Was it anger or pain that fueled his singular burst of effort on my behalf? Was it the only way he could hurt the woman he loved but who no longer loved him in return?

I don't expect I'll ever get an answer for any of these questions. I don't imagine the details of nearly forty years ago are as set in stone for them as for my mother.

Still, I love them all. I love my family for giving me a happy life, for teaching me compassion and humor. For keeping me innocent for as long as they could. I have no choice in the matter. I'm too old now to be angry like I might once have been. I don't know what they were thinking when these events unfolded, in the summer of 1979, but I choose to believe that everyone involved did their best to love and protect me.

Just let me still think the best about everyone. Let me believe it was all a huge, forgivable mistake. Let me leave it behind. I am tired of feeling sad over things I couldn't control. Let me still choose to believe that, for all of it, I've been lucky.

Bread Lies

It was a Christian Ladies' Luncheon. The invitation, handmade and hand-delivered a week prior, had said just that. The host, Lila, was more moneyed than most of her guests, and she made it a point to remind them with the gaudy display of meticulously arranged tea sandwiches, polished carnival glass, and an abundance of white lace décor that matched the invitation she'd dropped into our mailbox. None of it made much sense together, in rural 1980s Oregon, but the point was made. She had done her research.

Why was I there?

I suppose I had nothing else to do. And I would have been bored at home, pestering my grandfather and the ranch hands as they worked and relaxed in the shade of summer. It's possible that I insisted on going when I heard that it would be at Lila's house. She was my grandmother's church friend and our down-the-road neighbor, a widow with the time and means to absolutely fill her house—every flat surface and windowsill in sight—with strange and sometimes beautiful ceramic oddities, except for the pristine dining room. Here she occasionally hosted gatherings of church friends and their children, or, in my case, grandchildren.

The other kids—three other boys—had been sent outside to do boy things, but I was allowed to remain indoors with my book so long as I was quiet while the ladies discussed church matters. The church proper was in need of new decorations, it seemed, and many people were in need of prayers. The place reeked of hairspray and store-bought potpourri.

I paid little attention to their conversation. My attention was divided between my book of Greek mythology and the array of small, carefully placed sandwiches on the buffet table across the room. The bread was of particular interest. There were three distinct types, three colors. The dark brown bread looked particularly delicious, like the kind my grandfather occasionally made at home, in the cast-iron skillet that was designated specifically for bread making and nothing else. I loved it. He made it with dark beer, a "secret ingredient" that I took much pleasure in knowing about. We would slather on butter and eat it throughout the day, tearing off handfuls like savages every time we passed through the kitchen. We never made sandwiches with it, though, and my curiosity was piqued. What a great idea. They had to be delicious, no matter what was in between the slices.

Lila talked on and on. She had such health problems. Her dogs had them, too. The neighbor kids stole things. The weather had been just unbearable. I wondered if the overpowering smells of her house were partly to blame for her woes. I just wanted the sandwiches.

At last she invited everyone to partake. I knew not to rush the table first, but I would take no chance on losing out on the deliciousness I'd been eyeing for most of an hour. I waited for my grandmother's look of "permission granted" to approach, but I would beat the other boys, who hadn't been called inside yet, to the table.

The first of the ladies had made her way over, and my grandmother had given me the go-ahead. I snatched up two of the dark brown sandwiches and bit off a third of one before I'd returned to my seat. Bad manners, to be sure, but I was ravenous.

It didn't taste how I expected it to. And as I chewed I became aware of an entirely unexpected flavor assaulting me from within: the cloying, medicinal taste of ground caraway seed. It was rye. Dreaded, reviled rye bread.

My mouth stopped working, and I looked around hoping to remain unnoticed as I found something—anything—to spit the foulness into rather than swallow it. As I searched, I made eye contact once more with my grandmother. She also had one of the traitorous sandwiches on her plate. She knew. Her eyes bored into me with a look of *do not dare.*

The taste was so terrible—somewhere between potting soil and Band-Aid adhesive (don't ask how I know that flavor). She knew how much I hated it. I had refused it before, on several occasions, loudly. In a moment, once the inevitability of my situation reached critical mass, the partially chewed sandwich would be a regurgitated blob on my plate. The ladies of the luncheon would never be the same. They'd be scarred and scandalized forever by my disgusting act, and I would never again be allowed to leave the confines of my own home. I would live as a prisoner, a pouty hermit whose only company would be grandparents still ashamed, still outraged by The Thing I Did At The Luncheon That One Time.

"We shall not speak of it," I imagine my now-imperious grandmother saying as she clicks and bolts the many locks on my bedroom door (barred and made of iron, naturally) every night for the rest of my life.

But my grandmother was too quick for that, and well skilled in dealing with children, especially me. She was on it. She was up and over to me in a perfumed flash—smiling, conversing. And in a single deft motion the remaining sandwich on my plate was gone, as were the recent contents of my mouth—both swept with a sure hand into the recesses of her shiny white purse. No one appeared to have noticed. It never happened. The purse, and the quicksilver thinking of its owner, had saved us all.

I was tempted, briefly, to return to the buffet table in search of other, better things. I didn't, though, and the look I received as I eyed the table reinforced my decision to stay put. I returned to my book. It seemed safer—wiser—to eat things at home, where sandwiches told the truth and I knew what I was swallowing.

Things I'd Need

There's nothing like permanent loss to remind you of all the things you've left behind and wish you hadn't, no matter how illogical the notion of holding on to them.

I miss driving on muddy back roads with my grandfather to check on missing livestock, to inspect some crumbling old tree that had been struck by lightning, to check out the gigantic hornets' nest that had been built in the barn. He spoke to me like an adult, especially when out of my grandmother's earshot, and when we were alone he would break down the reality of whatever situation was currently in play for me like I was a grownup, almost the polar opposite of my grandmother's natural inclination to sugarcoat and shelter. He had a wicked sense of humor, and I'm guessing that at least partially, I inherited my sailor mouth from him.

I miss watching '80s cartoons with my grandmother. She was surprisingly intrigued by them—the more fantastical, the better. I'd get off the bus from school, and as soon as *M.A.S.H.* was over (how I hated *M.A.S.H.*) a two-hour animation block would start. She'd make us popcorn and we'd nerd out together, watching quietly as some serious shit went down on screen. Her personal favorite was *ThunderCats*. Years later, when I was a college student, I told her I wanted to write. She said, "Write something like the ThunderCats."

Being raised by older people means you are raised by frequently exhausted people. My grandparents were both tireless workers who always had too much to do, even without me added to the workload. There was always some household project to get to, some animal to be especially cared for.

My grandmother did *everything* for so long, managing every financial aspect of a working ranch, caring for the multitude of pets and livestock that inhabited the place, raising and dealing with me and whichever other grandchild she'd been tasked with for the day or week, playing mother to the world at large. All the while, through all of the years of her life, the damage inflicted by her own upbringing had gone largely ignored.

By the time I was eight or nine it had caught up with her. Her disposition changed, though her love for me never did. She carried with her a look of internal distress that marred her otherwise cherubic features. There were times when she seemed near some kind of psychological collapse, where she seemed perpetually on the verge of tears or a sudden storm of rage at some random target, often enough her husband or her children. I never could understand if her anger toward them was legitimate or just a misdirection of her long-suppressed anger toward her parents, both dead by this point for several years. I wondered if their deaths had slowly allowed her to unlock the things she had kept hidden away out of that same sense of duty and love that governed her entire existence and, largely, her entire generation.

She was a product of an era in which "mental health" was unheard of. You got over it, whatever it was, and got on. You didn't lament the injustices done to you. You were grateful for food and shelter and your family, even if they were abusive and generally horrible. You were expected to be of service, especially if you were a woman.

She did her duty, such as it was. She suffered to keep the family together and comfortable. She never spoke ill of her father except to say that he was an alcoholic, but I have wondered throughout my life if the abuses she endured from him weren't far more extensive and terrible than she said they were. It would make sense, given her reluctance to keep the bad things hidden, swept under the rug along with any conflict or potential awkwardness that might accompany.

In my early teenage years, she would make the decision to help herself and seek a psychologist to aid her in sorting it all out. This caused much turmoil, as she was the lynchpin of the house. No one else was available or willing—or perhaps capable—of caring for me like she did, leaving something of a power vacuum as far as my authority figures were concerned.

The relative instability of my living situation (which really wasn't all that unstable, but I was a preteen and clearly in need of all the stability and structure I could get) made me even more unruly than before, and argumentative to a fault. At school I was meek. The aggression and scrutiny of other kids intimidated and embarrassed me. I wanted to hide and be left alone most of the time. But at home I was a combative, spoiled monster, which didn't help things in the least. I was frequently relegated to my room to "think about things." In reality it was to keep my temper and generally shitty disposition from sending my newly fragile grandmother over the edge. My aunts showed up more frequently than before, and I can only assume it was to wrangle me, the awful child who should have been sent back to his parents years ago.

There was talk for a few years of me going to live with one of my aunts, or with my father, but my grandmother judged neither situation ideal, though she herself was growing incapable of dealing with me at all. My grandfather tried, but his strengths were in hard, honest work and days spent away from the children for whom he did it all. He had no head for discipline, and I think that most of my outbursts and comparatively strange personality traits only confused him. He was loving but always operated best at a busy stone's throw away. I probably inherited that trait, looking back at my own adulthood. Maybe we all did.

The talk of my possible relocation died away swiftly. My grandmother couldn't let me go. Strangely, the one place I might have fit would have been with my mother, who had other children and a relatively stable life with her new husband. But never in any of the conversations we'd had about it was she mentioned to me as an option. Never once did anyone say her name. I wonder now if it was deliberate.

I stayed, and continued on with my poor grades and terrible behavior. It seemed that my list of parent figures was growing, with aunts and extended relatives nearby all the time as my grandmother attempted to cope with whatever trauma she had at last recognized within herself. My father, during this time, however, was absent.

The idyllic circumstances and routine of my young life had begun to unravel, starting with the strongest, most vital of threads.

◦━ ⚜ ━◦

The lumber mills began to decline as the '80s progressed. Forest products became a thing easily outsourced, bought from mills installed by American companies in other countries with a massively reduced

39

price tag. The workers worked for less than Americans, and the wood was easier to get.

The loggers and mill workers would blame the government, with its ever-tightening laws on the harvesting of old growth timber. They would blame "the environmentalists," as they were vehemently referred to. They were spoken of with general hated, these bored, nosy city dwellers and communally minded hippies who never ventured into the forests, had no connection with the trees and animals that they were ruining lives to preserve. It became something of a cold war: loggers and millworkers versus the environmental conservation movement. Rednecks and hillbillies versus flower children and reality-challenged elitist intellectuals to the media.

The local news was biased in favor of the mills, at least in my house, and my memories of the conflict are always shadowed by short clips of angry loggers speaking defiantly to a news crew from the front of their own homes, or at the end of a ramshackle picket line with their families, their tired-looking wives and shy children, condemning the wave of change that spelled misfortune for them with words spat like bullets.

The northern spotted owl's habitat was being destroyed by increasingly invasive logging of the old-growth forests that they nested in. Its "threatened" status would make it the figurehead of the conservation movement in the Pacific Northwest, and cartoonish effigies would be hung in sawmills and plastered on the backs of cars and trucks on bumper stickers with slogans like, "Save a logger... shoot a spotted owl."

I can't blame them. Their livelihoods were as much under threat as the trees that the owls made their homes in, but their lowbrow humor and aggression didn't do them any favors, especially in the media.

The mill owners took out huge newspaper ads in an attempt to convince voters to side with them. It didn't work, at least not in the way they intended. They made themselves out to be greedy tyrants who cared nothing for the plants and animals they destroyed to fuel their hunger for cash.

By the end of the decade the forest product industry was decimated, reduced to roughly 10 percent of its original productivity, more by its own doing than anything else. They blamed the owls and Greenpeace, but the truth was that logging jobs were long in decline, even before calls for environmental protection and species endangerment. The old-growth forests were diminishing, and machines took the place of men in the mills. The owls won. I remember our neighbor saying those exact words to my grandfather one morning. He had been drinking, and I could smell the alcohol on his breath from the next room. His face was flushed and dirty, and his head was bowed in defeat.

The nickel mine closed too, in 1987, due to long-standing pollution violations and poor management. Children at school spoke of it like someone important had died, but it didn't touch me. It didn't make it into our home. My grandparents had worked hard all their lives, ensuring that their children and grandchildren wouldn't have to. Surprise—we didn't. None of their brood would inherit their willingness to sacrifice, to break their backs in the name of family and "the good life," a term that was used frequently in my house. They did everything, my grandparents, for everyone. No one learned how to work hard. It could be classified as the downside of loving too much.

In any event, their hard-earned money provided a shield of sorts from the financial devastation that was creeping over the state. By the time high school had mercifully ended for me, the town was a ruin. It was almost a mockery of its former self, though only a decade prior it was still "a nice place to live." Businesses were closing, and people were leaving for better places with better and more abundant jobs. I didn't notice it at the time. I was preoccupied with the usual concerns of early adulthood: self-identity, figuring out sex, impressing people who didn't matter, etc.

People still live there, but they seem drab and sad. The town has yet to recover from the loss of industry. There are thousands like it across the country, small towns dying. For people like my grandparents, who lived their entire lives in them, it must feel like a different world entirely now.

⊷ ⚎⬦⚎ ⊶

When I left, no one tried to stop me. No one asked, "What if you stay?" or "How could you want to leave us?" They helped me pack. They gave me things I'd need, little keepsakes and kitchen implements. They gave me money, more of it than I'd ever seen or needed before.

My grandfather, as I loaded the last of things into my car, handed me a twenty-dollar bill. I already had an envelope full of cash that I'd been handed discreetly by my grandmother, so the gesture confused me.

"For gas. If you need to come home," he said, and his calloused hand gripped mine tightly for an instant before he sent me on my way. It echoed a thing my grandmother had said they day before as I was packing my belongings into boxes, unsure as to what I'd need and what I should leave behind:

41

"You can always come home, okay?"

I rarely visited after I left. It didn't feel like home anymore. It felt like someone else's memories, someone who'd been given a good start, a childhood filled to the brim with love and freedom, but never appreciated it enough and departed nonetheless.

I knew my grandparents missed me. I imagined them passing by my empty bedroom, catching a glimpse of my third-grade photo as they walked down the hall, or the silence when a visiting neighbor inquired as to my whereabouts and remarked on how they hadn't seen me in so many years. Every good memory I'd had with them would scroll across my mind's eye whenever I needed a reason to hate myself. The guilt became a barb embedded in my skin, another reason to disapprove of myself, another tool I used to torture myself. How could I have abandoned the only people who didn't abandon me?

My grandfather's health was declining. His eyesight was mostly gone, and his hearing was never great, a product of his many years of working around machines and chainsaws and unmuffled motors. He had begun experiencing strange pains in his sides and back that came and went. They debilitated him to the point where he'd sleep all day and sometimes all night as well. He couldn't describe what it felt like, and sometimes his stomach was so upset that he couldn't eat for days. He'd lost weight because of it, which at any other time in his life would have been a good thing.

I knew it as cancer before they did, I think. I didn't know right away how bad it was, but I had seen cancer enough times in my years of working in healthcare to know that's what it was. But no one in my family had been afflicted like this. It still felt like a joke or a misdiagnosis, even when it became obvious that his body was dying quickly. Maybe I hoped against logic that it was still a treatable ailment, still something one recovers from, or that he'd be the first to do so for being such a strong, robust man throughout his life. I knew better, but I couldn't see my way around a piece of my foundation dying in such a pitiful, undignified manner. I don't know how else I expected him to die. Fighting off a gang of railway bandits, perhaps, like the characters he venerated in his westerns. He'd kill every last one of them and save us all before succumbing to his injuries, and then only barely.

He could die like Paul Bunyan, with whom he shared a striking number of traits, including an ox named Babe—no joke, though she wasn't blue. He could have expired after using his broad shoulders and back to hold up a collapsing barn (that was also burning, of course) to allow the women and children trapped within to escape. Only then could he relent and die. A loveable hero's death.

He had been, in his youth, in the small town he spent his entire life in, a lesser-known deity of American folklore. People always told stories about him. Whenever I was identified as his grandchild I was given a new tale about him.

They talked about his hard-drinking days, during which he was known for whiskey and fighting, for digging up bottles of buried moonshine for everyone to drink, for dragging a fellow logger with a broken leg a mile uphill to safety. In one story heard (from my seventh-grade math teacher), he punched his opponent through a wall. Or so the story went. I never confirmed if it was true, but I loved it enough to believe it regardless. His physical strength and big heart were small-town legendary, and the story of his death should have been too.

I pushed for an urgent medical checkup. It felt like I was sending my own grandfather to his grave, as if holding off on a diagnosis would stave off his pain and nausea, would overturn the universe's verdict that mandated his body to eat itself.

I think my grandmother knew. For all of her abundant blind optimism, I think she knew this was something that wasn't going away. I think it was why, after so many years, she began working into our conversations the notion of me coming back.

You can always come home.

I couldn't, I said to her and to myself. I had a job, a home of my own now, a life that required me to be in Portland. I couldn't—wouldn't—uproot everything I'd worked for to take so many steps back.

By the time the cancer was confirmed it was well into metastasis and was classified as cancer of the multiple organ variety. He didn't have much time left by then, and he was kept on a heavy dose of meds that dulled the pain, along with his general awareness of things.

He was fading fast, and I knew it. Still I hesitated, and held off on making the five-hour drive to see him in his final days. I don't know why. I had seen cancer and death before, and I knew how it would end. Something in me refused, I suppose, to acknowledge that a part of my life's foundation was a finite thing—a mortal man whose strength had abandoned him, whose life was coming to a close.

Only when he was at last officially bedridden, being visited daily by the kindly hospice nurse whose daughter I had gone to school with, did the reality set in for me. By then he had held on for longer than anyone had anticipated. My grandmother, though she never said it directly, would imply that he was waiting for me. I don't know why I waited so long. Some primitive logic, some child's line of reasoning was at play in my mind, telling me that if I didn't see it myself or acknowledge that his time was almost up, then it wouldn't be. That my distance from the situation was keeping him tethered to his own life, somehow.

So stupid of me. So predictable, like a Lifetime "made for television" film from the '90s. *Just go, and do it soon*, my more logical side shouted at me.

I made the drive, knowing what I'd see at the end of it.

⊶ ⊫◊⊠ ⊷

He was happy even as death came to claim him, cracking barely comprehensible jokes and trying to keep up with whatever conversation was taking place around him. He was barely coherent, but he understood what was happening.

Somehow, he knew who I was and that I'd come home. I had feared that, in his highly medicated state, he wouldn't recognize me. I feared that the trip would be as bad as I was making it before I arrived. But he knew me.

Family members were everywhere, and neighbors and friends. The house was bursting with them, a disorganized line of goodbyes and well-wishes. I can't recall what any of them said to him, or to me. Of that final day I mostly remember my grandmother's face: mask-like and serene. No cracks showing. She was always good at that. Her faith sustains her in hard times. She'll see him again in heaven. Everyone she's lost, she'll see again someday.

I don't believe in heaven, or hell, or anything else I can't see. I never did. But if there is something after, some place that is a reward for a life of kindness, of honest valor, they both deserve to be there.

I stayed all day, in the house I grew up in. I didn't want to be there, but how could I leave? It was such a scene of sadness, of impending loss. It felt like a violation of all the good memories, like they had lodged a formal complaint in my brain. Eventually I'd have to go back to the life I had made for myself at my grandparents' insistence. A job. A boyfriend who had messaged me earlier that day to tell me that he'd have dinner ready for us when I got home. I had already warned him that my mental state would most likely be messy, at best. He didn't care, he said. He just wanted to help how he could.

"Papa. I'm going home," I said. His real name had been supplanted years prior by the designation of Papa. I don't know who called him that

44

first, but I doubt it was me. I stopped calling him that after I'd left the first time. It stopped fitting him, as I grew out of my own dependence on his care, and I couldn't refer to him as "grandpa" by the time he died.

He rested in sitting position in the railed hospital bed they had set up in the living room. The orange and amber stained-glass owl that had hung there for all my life had finally been moved to another lesser window to make room for the rolling entourage of apparatus that seems to follow the dying wherever they go—IV poles and trays of syringes and pills and extra pillows and pink plastic basins and stacks of crisp white towels that appear from seemingly nowhere.

His eyes were closed, his face strained, perhaps by pain, or perhaps from the effort of listening to everything around him and maintaining what grip he could on the present.

"I'll be here," he said, dreamily, and we both knew he wouldn't be. And I patted his arm and kissed him on the head like I might have any other time I'd come to visit and then gone home, and then I left again. I drove back to Portland, back up the interstate to the life I'd built, and four days later my brother called to tell me he was gone.

<hr>

I miss waking up in the morning to laughter from the dining room, where my grandmother and whoever had come for coffee sat, making jokes about their husbands or children or pets. The laughter would escalate in proportion to the offensiveness of the joke, and the amount of coffee drank. I loved it when my grandmother and her best friend, Donna, would cackle with a tone of mild sadism at the joke that was just told. Even if I never could hear enough of it to understand fully, it was still hilarious. Only in those morning hours, in the relative solitude of the kitchen table would that particular music be applied to their laughter.

I miss holidays in our house. My grandparents both especially loved Christmas and would go to great lengths to ensure that the holiday season was enjoyed by everyone. The house could probably be seen from the moon, blinking and flashing like some holiday distress beacon for Santa or the aliens or whoever else might be up there during the holiday season. My grandmother would stay up late, for some reason, and she'd let me stay up too. She always seemed a little sad on those nights, and I never figured out why, but I remember how peaceful the world seemed by the shifting colored lights of the tree, and I miss the anticipation of knowing that the house would soon be filled with friends and family and everyone would, for a day or two, be happy.

I miss hearing their secret conversations from the kitchen, when they didn't know I was listening. They seemed like different people when they were alone, more vulnerable, but also more honest and funnier. They'd make jokes that would never be made anywhere else, and flirt with each other in ways that would make me feel ashamed for listening, though I didn't stop. My grandmother would always say, "You behave yourself." He never did.

I miss the joyful, busy silence of that place. It was like they had cast a spell over the acreage, holding everything in a kind of peaceful, content stasis in which nothing terrible could enter or last for long. Just soft wind from the hills and the singing of frogs and crickets from the fields. It made leaving hard, and it made the world seem unbearably, immeasurably cruel once I'd ejected myself from their nest.

All of that effort. They chose it. All of that time and love for a child not their own.

When I became someone they struggled to understand, they still tried, and always encouraged me to be me.

My grandfather, for all of his "good old boy"-ness, was one of the first people to give me open support when I announced my homosexuality. He was utterly unimpressed.

"I thought you were gonna tell me you killed someone," he said with a chuckle. His eyesight was failing by then, and he stared blankly at the garden in the backyard as he said it. The dogs were dozing at his feet.

He squeezed my arm. His grip was still strong. He said, "Just live your life, son. Be happy. It's okay. Most everything is horseshit anyway." Then he returned to his Zane Gray novel, held comically close to his face even though it was a large print edition. He would lose his ability to read altogether in the coming year.

I owe my grandfather big for that encouragement. It was simple, just a few words, but they took on a greater meaning than he probably meant for them to.

A few days after he died, I stood in my own kitchen and told my then-boyfriend I'd marry him. A piece of me thought we were rushing into it; we'd only known each other for about a year. But he made me happy. So I recalled my grandfather's words and I said "okay" and now my then-boyfriend is my husband of a few years, asleep upstairs in our bed as I write this.

I'm sure my grandfather didn't specifically mean, "Get gay-married," or not exactly, but that's where it went, his support. I wanted to be happy and he had given me permission to.

My grandmother has lost much of her faculty and memory from a stroke. She remembers the good times only, now. I envy her, in a way.

All I know of compassion, of dutiful love, I know because of her. She is, at the bottom of it all, as much my mother as the woman who claims the title by genetics, and by the signature on the weathered birth certificate that I keep tucked in my dresser, in a sealed plastic bag like some fragile relic from a bygone era.

"You can always come home, okay?"

Those parting words still echo in my head when I'm lonely, or hopeless, or desperate. Why not? Leave it all behind. Say "fuck it" and pack my things. Go back to my weird bedroom, the one I'd painted emerald green against everyone's better judgment, the hue so bright you could see it from the edge of the fields at night like an inexplicable square of sunlit jungle in the dark. Go back to the quiet nights, frog and cricket-filled; to the vast star-filled skies; to the lowing of cows in the morning fog. Go back to unconditional, if misapplied love I left behind, that I want to believe still waits for me there.

YOUTH, GROUPED

In Briar Caves

The first time I saw another boy without his clothes, I was five. He was maybe a year or two older. A neighbor kid, but I don't remember his name. There were a few other kids there, all boys, all around the same age. I was, or perhaps simply felt, the smallest and youngest. We were in a cave made of briars.

The caves were, in truth, only a few yards of twisted tunnel that shaped themselves naturally in the middle of the blackberry briars. I'm not certain if "briar" is the correct term, botanically speaking. It might be "thicket" or "bramble" or maybe something else. We called them briars. They grew quickly and rampantly, a nuisance to farmers and landscapers, difficult to remove. The roots grow deep and can survive frigid weather, pesticides, complete destruction of the aboveground branches, even burning. Do what you will, the briars say. We'll be back next spring.

The mostly-straight line of thorny, dense blackberry bushes defined a quarter-mile border between my grandparents' property and that of the neighbors, having overtaken and grown along the line of now-subsumed fencing installed whenever the bounds of ownership were first established. They marked the edge of the land on which I was allowed to roam.

I grew up at the end of the "go outside and play" era, in the final few years before abductions and the horrors of child rape and murder had inundated the American consciousness. After school, and lunch, and

51

whatever other daily requirements were met, I was set free to wander the property within reason.

I always had dogs with me, my grandmother's silent caretakers. She told me often enough that she had instructed the dogs to watch out for me and to report back to her if I should break a rule. There weren't many: don't leave the property, don't burn anything, always come home when called. I eventually broke each of them at least once, but in my earliest memories I remember deliberately following her rules for fear of the dogs ratting me out when I got home.

Some of the tunnels had no end; others came out on the neighbor's side, and I never used those. The actual fencing had been destroyed, partially digested by the briars. Remnants were still visible in places—rotted posts jutting out of the ground like the crumbling ribs of a dinosaur, warped and rusted barbed-wire that mingled here and there, almost poetically, with tendrils of thorny briar, as though one mimicked the other.

In three adjacent places, the caves seemed to open up into small rooms. Holes in the top and sides let in sunlight, just enough of it to illuminate what would otherwise have been a terrifyingly dark place. In the larger "room," there was an old tree stump that had been torn from the ground and reworked into a seat, or a table. It might have been put there by my father and his friends in years prior. It had burn marks at the base, and dried reddish wax spilled and flaked down one side like old blood, which I always pretended it was.

This was the most difficult of the three to find, and the scariest to navigate to or from, even in the barest hint of encroaching evening darkness. I rarely stayed out late enough to see the sun begin to set, but once in late fall, when night comes sooner and sooner with every passing day, I lingered too long and had to find my way out in the dark. My jacket snagged on a jag of barbed fencing, and I fell. My face was scratched by a rogue blackberry thorn. For a moment, bleak terror dominated me. It fell over me like a heavy blanket and I lost all hope, all sense of sanity in the way that frightened children do. I would be trapped and lost forever in the caves, until someone thought to search for me there, by which time I'd already have starved or frozen to death.

The snuffling of the dogs, having doubled back for me, interrupted the unfolding of my short life and death. I pulled myself upright and followed their wagging tails to the entrance. When my grandmother asked me about the long red line running from nose to ear, I told her I accidentally ran into the screen door so she wouldn't ban me from the caves.

There are dogs in all of my earliest memories, waiting at my feet for something to happen, barking in alarm or elation at something, running ahead of me as I follow them, breathless. Oddly, I've never had one of my own since I left that place.

I wish I could remember more of the conversation that led a neighbor boy I barely knew to completely disrobe in front of me and three other boys. That seems like an important part of the story, but it's gone. I do recall a discussion about how all boys had the same parts and how girls didn't have parts at all:

"All boys are made the same. My mom told me so." From the boy I knew the best, the one whose house was on the other side of the briars, whose grandparents were friends with mine.

"Not all boys." From someone else in attendance.

"That's not true! You're talking about girls' parts."

I don't remember saying anything. I was terribly nervous. It felt like everyone else had these conversations on the regular, but no one ever did in my family. These were questions to be answered in whispered private, indoors, though I was not yet brave enough to whisper them in my house.

It was hastily decided, with downcast eyes and lowered voices, that there was only one way to know for sure.

Each of the other three boys unzipped their pants and pulled them down just enough to expose themselves. Eye contact was not made by anyone. They just stared at the ground, pants below buttocks, held tightly in their hands as if they might slip off. I stood back and watched in silence. No one asked me to do the same at first, so I didn't move. Glowing red coals burned my stomach and lungs. The dogs were uninterested.

There were bottle caps and empty cigarette packs scattered on the ground, the occasional jag of brown glass, the odd playing card. I remember turning a jack of spades over with my foot when I saw the boys begin to unzip their jeans, to keep him from witnessing the act and telling my grandmother. She would have reacted badly, I knew, and I felt a surge of something like rebellion at the knowledge that I would never tell her.

The older boy, taller and more brazen than the rest of us, stared at me for a moment. He seemed empowered by the level of exposure in the room. His eyes didn't leave mine for a long moment as he pulled off his shoes, his pants, his underwear, leaving on his white tube socks with mint-green bands at the tops. He pulled off his ball cap too, and finally his shirt, hanging it on a low rope of briar behind him.

He turned to face us with a look that could have been pride or defiance. His sudden nudity seemed to absorb all sound from the little room. His body was more advanced than the rest of ours, though probably less so than I remember. To the eyes of a child he seemed like a fully grown man. Something I would never be.

He stared at me, at the other boys, all of us stunned or perhaps transfixed. The dogs lounged and sniffed at the ground absently, waiting.

"What about you?" he asked me.

He was right; I had agreed. I stared at the dirt floor of the cave and unzipped my pants. They were bronze-colored corduroy. Nothing changed as I did it, but I saw my grandmother in my mind, ashamed.

No one spoke for what seemed like hours. We stood, staring at this naked boy, taller and blonder than the rest of us. He seemed to soak it up, like we had asked him to do it and he had rewarded us. A lawn mower sputtered nearby. A car crossed the "singing" metal bridge on the other side of the property, alerting the dogs. They bolted out of the caves to inspect the arrival, breaking the spell of paralysis we had unwittingly cast.

I was first to pull my pants back up. The other boys followed suit. The older boy stood and watched us all, still naked except for his tall socks, and then finally pulled his clothes back on as we watched.

"You're not gonna tell anyone, right?" He stood close.

I shook my head no. My mouth refused to form the word. We left the caves in a single-file line, and it was unanimously agreed upon that all boys were, essentially, made the same.

I don't recall ever speaking of the strange event again, to anyone. But every memory of being in the caves after the incident with the other boys is of me alone. Not even the dogs are with me in later recollections. I can't say why.

Like much of my childhood landscape, the briar caves no longer exist. My grandfather, never to be outdone in his work, finally decided to be rid of them. They had grown too far inward, into the property. It was a waste of space that could be used for other, more lucrative purposes. He burned them. They came back. He swore at them (he swore at everything) and hired a man on a bulldozer to plow them down, scouring the earth beneath of the tenacious roots. They didn't come back after that.

I was an adult by this time, long gone from that place. It seemed like a violation when I visited and was greeted by open field, a flat space of green and straight, sturdy lines of new fencing where the caves had once been. It stung me to see the neighbor's side of the field, to see their squat little ranch house looking back at me in the distance, previously obscured, as my own had been to them. It infuriated me to think that one of my memories was now just that and nothing else. It changed the dynamic of my holiday visit, I recall. My grandmother and grandfather both commented that week on my mood, on how "sullen" I seemed, though I had a long history of sullen moods with no apparent explanation.

All I had felt as the boy took off his clothes was a pang of unfamiliar longing, for what I couldn't tell. Did I want to be him? Or did I want him to stay and remain unclothed? I had expected to feel shame as he removed his clothes, or disgust, but there was none to be found. My eyes had been solidly fixed on his naked form until it wasn't naked anymore, waiting for something I couldn't explain. The other boys exposing themselves in the cave, me doing the same, and the obvious impropriety of it all seemed trivial by comparison. The caves had shielded us from prying eyes, and from whatever intervening sense of logic the outside world might have imposed on the events of that day.

One Night Only

The first period of the day was "Health." A ridiculous name for what we were expected to learn; it should have been called "Basic Human Hygiene/Biology/Psychology and Also How Sex Parts Work." The teacher of the class was Ms. Smythe, an emotionless rake of a woman who dressed far too well for her post and had been in the employ of the school for so long that my father could recall being instructed by her in the archaic ways of the typewriter in the years before she was reincarnated by the magic of the public education system into an instructor of Health.

I sat in the second-to-back row, staring at nothing while Ms. Smythe pointed to leg bones and cell walls and secretory glands and metabolic charts. I think I passed with a C, which was more than I deserved, given how little I tried or cared in first period, in eighth grade, and in school, generally. Everything was boring or too difficult. I preferred to read books about ancient history, about UFOs, about places I'd never see in real life because they were fictional or so far away that they might as well be. I imagined splitting myself into two Dustins, one subservient to the other. That one would go to Health class. The other one, the real me, would stay in bed and fucking sleep as long as I wanted. My grandparents wouldn't know I was still in bed, and at the end of the school day the clone-me would come home. We would re-assimilate, and all of his acquired knowledge, every boring bit of required knowledge, would be mine. Naturally, he'd be a better traditional learner than I ever was.

I never spoke to anyone in that class. If being the weird, vaguely antisocial kid who generally hated school wasn't enough, I was also not an early riser (and I am still not an early riser). The fog of sleep had never fully left me until well after Health had concluded for the day. But one morning Ms. Smythe came to class wearing a black-and-white striped pantsuit. It must have been tailored; no pantsuit straight from the rack could have possibly molded to her bony frame so well. Her salt-and-pepper hair was swept up and back in the tall-but-rounded fashion of the early-1990s middle-aged lady. As she turned to erase equations from the chalkboard, someone's finger poked me in the backpack.

"Beetlejuice, Beetlejuice, Beetlejuice!" Patrick whispered. It was the first thing he'd ever said to me.

In truth, Patrick B. was probably less beautiful than I recall, but in the early light of my first class of the day he was a tawny, lanky beacon of masculine perfection. Though he was the same age and size as me, he seemed infinitely "bigger," infinitely more present and capable than I could ever be. His hair was one shade away from true blond, effortlessly floppy and just the right amount of messy, like he'd woken up too late, tried to style it, and had given up halfway and rushed out the door to class. It worked. I stared at his hair frequently, wondering if that look might work for me as well. He wore a lot of denim. It was always a bit too big for him, and his limbs and lean torso would show through if he turned or stretched right, sending a fully charged electric eel that I always tried my best to ignore racing through the dark water of my insides.

His heavy-lidded eyes were a clear blue. I had envied light eyes for most of my life. No one in my family had them except my mother, who was gone, like something vaguely angelic or an alien being who had been forced to return to her home world without me. Those eyes seemed special and luminous, though many people I despised in that school had them too. Patrick wore them better, gave them something the other students did not.

He had something else too, some quality that the other kids didn't. Or perhaps he lacked something. He could hold a conversation without ridiculing or bullying or bragging. He understood sarcasm, which I was already fluent in. I was attracted to him immediately, as soon as his finger made contact with my backpack, though I had never noticed him before.

I knew by this time that I was probably gay. Or possibly just bisexual, which sounded better to me (and safer, somehow). Or maybe I was some other version of *not straight* that I didn't have a word for yet. But the knowledge was fleeting. I equated it, inwardly glowing with self-professed brilliance at the analogy, with the Loch Ness Monster. I

58

had read a book about it: mysterious, fascinating, enormous, potentially horrifying. My sexuality was the same: breaching the surface of my awareness just long enough for an occasional grainy photo to be snapped before it would descend once again into the inky depths of boyhood oblivion. Some piece of me kept saying *deal with it later*, so the knowing became easier and easier to forget until I was at school, where every boy in sight was beginning the metamorphosis into manhood, and I would find myself staring too long, imagining things I didn't know were actual things, forcing myself to laugh at jokes that weren't all that funny. Girls did the same thing and were rewarded for it, but no one appeared to notice when I did it.

Except Patrick, I told myself after the Beetlejuice incident. *He sees me*. I think I heard that line in a movie. We became friends—or at least friendly, which was the same thing to me, lacking the experience to know that a difference existed. I was shy and nervous about most things, intimidated by every aspect of the middle school existence that was so violently different from my life at home. I was probably difficult to talk to, but Patrick seemed not to notice, or perhaps just not to care. We never spent any time together outside of school, but it felt good to tell myself that I had at least one person on my side, someone who shared a few of my sentiments.

I knew relatively little about him, but when prompted by my grandmother for information on "friends," his name was the first to be mentioned. On hearing his last name, she shocked me with her knowledge of him; she knew more than I did. His father, it happened, was a minister of the little church in the middle of our little town, the one where people cried and danced in the aisles as Christian rock music blared so loudly from the open doors of the place that you could hear it all the way up on Main Street.

"It's too much for me," she said.

No dancing at Grandma's church. The people she congregated with at her tiny red church on the hill in the neighboring town were much like her: sweet-faced, smiling even when there seemed to be nothing to smile at, confused and wounded by the world's hard edges, the ambivalent threads of cruelty that run through all avenues of life, touching everyone in one way or another. She would ask me, on occasion, to join her for the Sunday sermon. Her fellow parishioners—her friends—they missed me, she'd say. They hadn't set eyes on me since I was five, so I couldn't see how, but I felt pangs of guilt every time she brought it up. Not that it changed anything; it was never enough to make me go with her.

Past generations of my family had been devout. My great-grandparents had converted unused bedroom space into a tiny makeshift altar for the odd days when they couldn't make it to church. But the family's piousness had dwindled in recent years. By the time I was born, the only person still attending sermons was my grandmother, so naïve and kind of heart that by rights she was less suited to her position as the de facto matriarch of my family and more to the shielding and confined bliss of a nunnery.

The day my grandmother was baptized (as my mother recounted it to me), she'd come home soaking wet, her cropped and curly hair drooping, her makeup running like someone had tried to drown her but failed. But there was a glow in her face, a profound happiness that emanated from her after having been dunked in a lukewarm tub of water. She now saw the world with new, spiritual eyes, it seemed. She had found her home.

Did it trouble her to see everyone she loved fall away from the thing she placed so much of her faith in? Everyone else had reached some level of disillusionment with the church or with God and His rules for living well. Public opinion ranged from my father's ever-diplomatic "It was more relevant in BC times" to my grandfather's "Horseshit," which often enough earned him an equally public reprimand from his wife, a rarity reserved for only the most grievous of offenses. He had no taste for people, generally, and especially not in situations outside his comfort zone like a tiny rural church where he couldn't swear and laugh inappropriately without looks.

⋆⋅ ☳✦☶ ⋅⋆

The poster directly across the hall from my locker said, "Let's Talk About Jesus." The other posters in the wire-meshed windows were small ads for upcoming extracurricular events or for the newest young adult novels. But the Jesus poster was hung prominently, almost ominously on the tall windows of the library, slightly higher than the others. Odd placement, I thought, for something so unrelated to literature as I understood it.

It featured a very Caucasian messiah with blue eyes—not unlike Patrick's—that made contact with my own every time I switched books for my next class. The neon greens and oranges, the faux-haphazard chalkboard font, they were proof that Jesus was cool now. His rosy-cheeked face was jovial, like he wanted to laugh and he wanted everyone else to laugh with him. Gone was the aloofly kind-yet-stern-faced Jesus I'd seen in the portraits and candles in my grandmother's house for as

60

long as I could remember, and on the billboard along the interstate next to the truck stop, imploring women to keep their unwanted fetuses. God will provide, after all, and your babies want to be born, Jesus said. He said it with his eyes, with a look that said, *you know this already*.

I didn't know; I was just thirteen a month prior. I knew next to nothing of the world of adults, or of unwanted children, or of Jesus. I didn't want to know. Adults were angry and sad. They forced me and themselves to do all kinds of shit that none of us liked. They hated themselves, it seemed, and they wanted me to hate myself too.

On one Friday afternoon, after my last class had ended, as I tried to get in and out of the locker annex without Jesus looking at me, Patrick approached. I don't recall if I greeted him, but I do recall standing up straighter than I ever had when I saw him. I tried to look like something better than I was. I tried to fold myself inward, to appear small and not chubby. I held my face immobile, focusing on the shape of my mouth and hoping that he would too. I recall the quickening of my heart, like something important was about to happen and my insides were telling me not to fuck it up. I probably looked sick, or afraid.

"Me and a bunch of kids are gonna meet at my dad's church tonight. Wanna come?"

Effortless, nonchalant friendliness. This seemed unusual. I assumed that some toll would eventually be required of me. Other kids my age were a mystery, and often a treacherous one. I didn't understand what they did with themselves when they weren't at school. Did they retreat into solitude like I did, into that world that was all mine? Or were they all somehow still together, perpetually gossiping and talking about sex in unrealistic ways like I heard them do all day at school? Other kids wanted money, or they wanted me to laugh at their terrible jokes and play pranks on teachers like we were in some cartoon where the punishment, if there ever was to be a punishment, rarely fit the crime. They seemed to be constantly trying to draw attention to themselves, when usually I was aiming for the opposite.

But Patrick simply conversed, like the adults I was surrounded by at home, and to whom I could talk with more ease. Like he was actually interested. My response came slowly.

"I'll have to ask my grandma," I said. For permission? I never asked permission for anything. I had no need to, but it seemed like the right thing to say.

"I can call your house and ask for you if you want."

Anxiety. *No, I certainly do not want that. My behavior will betray me. They'll see the change in me. They'll see the hungry, hopelessly devoted look on my face and know the truth immediately. The questions and whispers that follow will follow me forever. I will be branded as all of the things I get called at school. I will get AIDS and be a faggot and my family will cast me out into the streets. All because I think you're beautiful.*

"It'll be fine. My family's cool," I told him. I didn't believe it, not at all. "Cool" meant permissive, of course, though I had no idea what they'd say about something like this.

He gave me directions. I accepted them in silence. I knew exactly where the church was; I saw it every day on my way home from school. Anything to prolong our interactions. Anything to keep his eyes fixed on mine for a moment longer.

Later that day another girl asked me if I'd be at the "youth group." I had never heard those words before, but yes, I'd be there. *Patrick invited me personally.* I didn't say it out loud, but to the even-slightly-trained eye I was most likely beaming like I'd just been asked to prom by the captain of the football team. Beautiful Patrick B. wanted to see me, more of me than a groggy first-period class at the crack of dawn. He wanted to know me, and I was ready to be known.

Eel again. Stop that. Later.

Knowing what I did about his family, it should have come as no surprise to me that Patrick would at some point attempt to indoctrinate me into his family's faith. I told myself that churches were churches. But I knew almost nothing of religion. I knew that Adam and Eve had had it really good. Then one day Eve grew defiant (or was tricked, depending on whom you ask) and ate a piece of fruit (which fruit was the forbidden one?) from the wrong tree, and then everything went to absolute shit and now there's war and disease and people suffer endlessly and then they die.

I knew about Noah's ark, which made zero sense. I'd read in an issue of *The Sun* that it had been found, at long last, on a mountain in Turkey. I remembered something in a story from the single Bible-centric book in my collection about a woman fleeing a burning city with her family. God told her not to look back, but she did—because how could you not?—and was promptly transformed into a pillar of salt. Not as epic as it could've been, this transmogrification, but I suppose it would have been to humans from an age of the world less desensitized, before comic books and video games and horror films made vengeful acts of the divine into an art form to be outdone, over and over.

That was it, the full extent of my theological knowledge. I cared nothing for Jesus, who had stayed out of the way, watching from the sidelines with disinterest as I slowly grew into understanding my "alternative lifestyle" (a term people actually used in 1991). I wanted nothing more to do with religion. I just wanted to be near Patrick, all the time, and when I was alone my thoughts took other turns. I imagined what it would feel like to lie in a bed with him, to touch his lips with my own, to put my hands underneath the loose denim of his jeans. It seemed profane, and I knew never to speak of it. I saved those thoughts for my bedroom and nowhere else, locked away in a box of secrets I believed hidden from the rest of the world, though other kids already called me "faggot" and "queer-bait" (whatever that means—if you know, please message me). A few had asked me if I had AIDS, but I still didn't know what exactly that was. Health class had not yet reached the "Horrors of STDs" module.

My father drove me into town. He asked me if I was meeting a girl. I said there'd probably be several, and he laughed as if to say, "Pace yourself."

I had received very little protest and surprisingly few questions that evening when I announced my intention to take part in a social activity in town. *In town* was a noteworthy thing—my grandparents' ranch, the seat of all family activity and my home, was eight miles out of it, and I was too young to drive. Other kids my age might have arranged rides with other, older attendees, but I had no one but my family to shuttle me to the recently remodeled church with the bright pink paint, where Patrick waited for me.

"Youth group... sounds loud," my father had said between bites of carrot cake left over from a birthday party. He stood in the middle of my grandparents' kitchen, eating on his feet like he still does, dressed like he just finished painting a house or installing metal pipes into something. It was a rare moment of involvement for him. He wasn't always around, but had shown up that morning, before I'd woken up, drinking coffee in the dining room and laughing like he'd been there all along. I never questioned it then, and have long since given up on understanding the multitude of dad quirks that define him.

"It's just a few kids." In truth, I hadn't a clue as to the number of attendees that evening. None of them mattered except one, and he wanted me there. The eel in my gut lurched again and I had to sit down.

I had expected at least a token show of resistance to the idea of me leaving the nest for an entire evening, which I almost never did. I was prepared to answer questions, but none came, other than arrival and departure times. Maybe they were just happy that I had finally decided to stop being the weird kid who spent all day in his room doing *something*.

I had also expected some level of elation, however suppressed, from my grandmother, but none came. Only many years later I would recall my father's face as he silently implored her to be stoic about it. I imagine that she was overjoyed that I'd found my way to Jesus on my own.

My father was wise enough to drop me inconspicuously on the corner before I had to ask. The door was open, so I entered into the church. It had been a few years since I'd seen the inside of one. I felt like an unwelcome presence, greeted by uncomfortable silence for my intrusion. Everything was made of the same wood that gleamed. A pink-and-white satin tapestry hung from the stage at the front of the room. There was a cross at each corner, and the words "ALL THINGS ARE POSSIBLE" were stacked in the middle of the thing, too small, and so close together as to be resting on top of each other.

A pair of women came from behind the stage and jumped slightly to see me standing there.

"You're here for youth group? You're early," one of them said. I was exactly on time, right at the beginning of the window of arrival time that Patrick had given me in his instructions that morning.

I was led through the door they'd just come out of, to a convention hall of sorts, attached to the back of the church under a long line of maple trees, hidden from street view completely. It felt threatening, somehow, to know that the church hid a secret building, even if it was probably only a secret to me.

I sat and fidgeted while the two women and a few other adults bustled about the place and asked me questions about myself as they passed— my name and age, where I lived, if my family attended services there. One of them, a frizzy-haired woman with a squeaky, nasal laugh and teeth that seemed too long for her head asked me about my relationship with God. I had never given it any thought, so I said it was fine. *God has relationships?*

She smiled wider and carried on with her setting up of things: chairs and small tables, stacks of plastic cups, assorted sugary beverages in coolers with the contents written in colored bubble letters on papers taped to each one. Our conversation was finished. I had passed some form of test, it seemed. She didn't need to know that I had cheated.

Other students arrived. A few greeted me, but the majority did not. We sat together at one of the tables, and I laughed when they did. Strange feeling, to be a part of their circle when I spent all day in their company feeling completely alone.

Patrick arrived late, and I felt like I could breathe again when I saw him get out of his brother's car. His older brother, Brandon, was so cool that I couldn't look directly at him for fear that my unworthy eyes would explode out of their sockets with a blast of fire. He was almost as attractive as Patrick, but he lacked the casual, friendly air of his younger sibling. He spoke to everyone like he was their kindergarten teacher or their psychiatric nurse. He wore shredded jean shorts that showed off his tanned and muscled legs and had tall, sculpted bleach-blond hair that could only have been taken out of the Vanilla Ice Manual of Style. He wore his sunglasses indoors, and also at night, I imagined.

He didn't recognize me, and immediately made it a point to introduce himself. He followed this with a rapid-fire barrage of questions similar to those asked by the frizzy-haired woman who'd welcomed me in. He followed those questions by turning me, physically turning me by gripping my shoulders, and loudly introducing me to the entire congregation like they didn't already know who I was. Many of us had gone through the entirety of grade school together. It hadn't made our connection any stronger. As he pushed me forward, I died a little.

Games commenced. First trust-falling, which I declined to play due to it being fucking insane, though everyone else seemed to enjoy it. I remember envisioning one of the fallers bashing their head open on the hardwood floor of the event hall and everyone expecting Jesus to fix it.

There was a three-legged race. Of course there was. I was volunteered by the frizzy-haired woman to be tied to Patrick. She probably did it because I hung back when the other kids were pairing off, which they did almost immediately, like they had planned for the race in advance. I hated pairing off, generally. But hesitating had paid off this time, and Patrick didn't seem to mind being tied to me.

I found it difficult to breathe, even before we started to run. As our legs were strapped together and his thing bumped against mine, I could feel my heart drumming all the way up to my brain and in the tips of my toes.

His closeness, the leather-and-straw smell of him, was disconcerting. My face grew hot, and the heat spread to the rest of me in the worst and best way. The thought of someone noticing was enough to inspire a panic that paralyzed my legs and made us nearly fall. When his hand grabbed mine for balance my heart lurched, almost painfully, in my throat. We came in last because of me. I was barely winded, but I pretended to be out of breath from the race to mask what was happening in my chest and head and pants. A girl from school commented that I needed more exercise if a simple game of Three-Legged Race was enough to tire me. I agreed; I was too lazy. The laughter that followed distracted me from Patrick as he untied us. I had hoped he would simply forget to.

It was all fun enough, safe enough, normal enough. Everyone there seemed to be in extraordinarily high spirits, in glaring contrast to the surly, cantankerous, tired faces I saw every day at school on the same bunch of kids. Some of them were the same ones who had called me horrible, confusing names and ask if I wanted a "sex change," but I was too new to being social to hold a grudge. Maybe I was mean at school, too.

I felt good about my decision to break free of my bedroom, my home, my self-imposed solitude. Until the final game commenced: Bible Trivia.

Teams of five or six were gathered at the flimsy tables. I wasn't on Patrick's team. It annoyed me, but I could do nothing about it. We moved our colored tokens around a board bearing symbols of faith: crosses with deflated-looking men hung upon them, their faces all hidden in shadow; desert travelers, robed and hooded against the storm on the horizon; a strange assortment of animals—refugees from the ark?—all looking fearfully skyward, waiting for something bad to happen. Every question was more confusing than the last. Any scrap of knowledge I possessed was useless.

Patrick was a star. I watched him as he mingled and shook hands, played a round or two of every game. He knew every person's name. He was born for this. He walked past me as I failed miserably at Jesus Trivia and smiled.

"You're doing great."

It encouraged me but had no effect on my Bible knowledge. I silently lamented the lack of "real" trivia questions that would have allowed me to demonstrate that I did, in fact, know things. Like: Which ancient culture invented toilet tissue? (China.) Which snail's name is also a color? (Periwinkle.) What species of snake did Cleopatra kill herself with? (Trick question! She didn't. She died from a poison made of opium and hemlock.)

As the game dragged on, something was happening in the church proper—a shuffling, a low rumble of movement and chatter. The focus of the adults seemed to shift to the new sounds in the adjoining room.

Brandon reappeared. He walked a full circle around the gathering of overexcited preteens, then clapped and whistled to gain our attention. It worked. The room fell silent almost immediately. His white denim jacket was off, and I found myself unable to look away from the skin of his incredibly toned arms.

"We have a special treat for everyone!" he said, eyes glassy with anticipation and pride. He directed us to leave whatever we were doing and follow his lead into the church.

We moved single file, like inmates, from one stuffy room to the next. The wood of the church smelled overpoweringly of artificial citrus from the just-applied spray polish. Like my own house, I realized. The pews gleamed with lemony cleanliness. I could see that no one knew what would happen next, except for Patrick and Brandon and some of the adults. The glint in his eye from a sidelong glance at me, his smirk, the straightness of his back—all said, *I've done good.*

The front double doors of the church opened, both at once, dramatically, and for a moment I believed that Jesus Christ was the special guest of the evening. Maybe He had finally come back from wherever He'd gone after the events disclosed in the Bible. Maybe I had been too busy with school and avoiding school and fantasizing about boys to notice. But no blinding heavenly light issued forth from the opened doors, like one would expect from the returning messiah's entrance. It was just a man, walking slowly into the church with a slow swagger that implied he was no stranger to an audience.

He was a traveling man of God, adorned in a sparkling blue jacket with sequins woven into crosses on the front and back. He couldn't have been a day younger than fifty-five, but he walked up the center aisle like Elvis Presley, pre-pills and banana-bacon sandwiches. Strapped to his back was a horned Gibson guitar, glossy blue like the jacket. His presence brought gasps from the audience, then a reverent hush as he took his place on the stage.

Following him was the smallest boy in the gathering, lumbering red-faced as he carried the man's amplifier up to the stage. He nearly lost his grip on the thing when he tripped on the electrical cord dragging on the ground, and everyone gasped, but no one moved to help him. His face went almost purple as he collected himself and proceeded to the stage.

The lights dimmed, and the traveling man stood silently as a spotlight was trained on him. His jacket sparkled, and the oily sheen of his skin almost matched the shine of the guitar he tuned. The other kids cheered and gasped. They knew him.

"There's a lot of love for the Lord in this room tonight," he said, and began to strum. He sang, first quietly, then at a volume that made the microphone obsolete. Tinny backup music streamed out from behind him. The crowd began to chant and sing along. Some of them prayed in small circles, mumbling with held hands and eyes fixed unblinking on the man as he sang.

The songs were forgettable, all geared toward young people in clear need of guidance in a world that seeks to corrupt, to ruin. Don't lie to your parents, don't cheat on schoolwork, and certainly don't think sexual thoughts, early teenagers. Jesus has rewards in store for the faithful, for those who abstain from sex and avoid all thoughts of it until marriage; those who avoid drugs and cigarettes and other things that stain and diminish the soul, somehow; those who get good grades in the name of the Lord, He who absolutely loves a squeaky-clean report card. He sang on, and played to the tune of the prerecorded music coming from his amp, his snakeskin boots tapping in time on the little stage.

He didn't mention in his songs what one should do if the mere thought of another boy in your first-period Health class makes you want to claw out of your own clothes and pounce on him like a hungry velociraptor. I wondered if he had special songs for that line of thinking. I imagined the extra level of disapproval on his face (and Jesus's) when he sang them. I imagined the titles: "To Get to Heaven, Go Straight" or "Jesus Says No (to Kissin' Other Boys)."

His head twitched and his eyes went wide like he'd seen something terrifying. His spun in circles. He spoke in tongues. I had never heard anything like it, though I'd read about it in a book on ancient religions. The oracles of antiquity had done it, in drug-induced states of fervor and prophecy. Early Christian figures had as well, or had witnessed others doing it. But this was a musician, a middle-aged man who, but for the jacket and guitar and adoring fans, looked like someone my grandparents would invite over for lunch to discuss farming techniques.

He threw back his head and howled, ecstatic, his face aimed at the spotlight. The music increased in tempo and volume, and he motioned to the kids dancing in the front row. They rushed up to him, swaying and jumping to the beat of the music. One by one he tapped them, almost absentmindedly, on the forehead, singing and strumming all the while.

They shook and shouted and fell away, caught by others awaiting their turn. A few of the girls glanced back nervously, ensuring that someone was there to catch them before submitting themselves to the downward-striking force of God's love, transmitted through the hand of this glittering, sweating man. He looked tired but joyously vindicated in his mission to render these middle schoolers momentarily unconscious. His quota was quickly met, and one of the adults in attendance gestured at the kids onstage to return to the front row. The last girl to fall down had to pick herself up and leave the stage on foot. Her friends had forgotten to collect her.

The music continued on, even louder, and the man shook, possessed by unseen forces that resembled a seizure, similar to the one I'd seen years before when a neighbor boy had fallen from an apple tree onto his head. The man's eyes rolled back, all white. His mouth flopped open. His hands, fingers splayed, waved back and forth like he was signaling for help. I wondered for a moment if he'd gone too far and was now in the throes of an actual medical emergency.

"Oh-oh-oh! My-my-myeee!" he chanted.

"He's down in my feet! The Lord's in my feet!" he screamed.

And he danced even harder—an uncoordinated high-stepping jig, to the tune of the electric guitar he was no longer playing, to the prerecorded backup music miraculously coming from the organ that no one had touched. His boots came down on the stage with such force that I could feel the reverberation of each stomp from my seat. The audience was entranced, and the love I saw on their faces for him seemed somehow perverse and frightening. I suddenly longed for my books and notepads, and the silence of my bedroom, and the distant, endless commotion of the kitchen on the other side of the house. I longed for the simplicity and peaceful routine of helping to prepare dinner. I longed for the stupid, meaningless quarrels with my cousins and brothers that I'd once claimed were ruining everything.

The music stopped. The audience shrieked and wept their approval, and he soaked it up. He was spent, leaning against the never-played organ, his jacket shimmering in rhythm with his heaving breaths. The applause went on for eons. Brandon took the stage, putting an arm around the man's shoulder and silencing the crowd once more with a raised hand and a wide-eyed "shh" face.

"Let's thank our new friend for bringing the spirit of the Lord down to us tonight."

A boy my age wept openly next to me. His friends looked proud of him and patted his back and shoulders encouragingly. My head felt too hot.

Brandon led the assembly in a long-winded prayer about finding our way to Christ and staying "pure." I remember something threaded in the prayer about teenage pregnancy, which didn't seem to fit, but I knew it didn't apply to me, so I paid no attention. My head was bowed like everyone else's, but all I could think of was finding the quickest, least conspicuous exit. I was surrounded, though. My sudden departure would be questioned. I tried my best to be invisible, but Patrick found me.

His eyes were rimmed with red and shiny with tears, and he made no attempt to hide it. It made his blue eyes even bluer, and for a moment I wanted to stay again. He placed one of his hands on my shoulder and took my wrist with the other, gently guiding me to the front of the room where the traveling man sat on the steps of the stage, encircled by fans asking for advice and autographs. He had a stack of tiny Bibles, like the ones issued in jail, that he signed on the inside back cover with a red marker. His blue jacket was unbuttoned, and his white undershirt was stained a sickly brownish yellow at the neck and armpits.

"Do you want to meet him?"

"No. I'm fine." I just wanted out, away from the man, from the praying and sobbing. Unconsciously, I jerked my arm from Patrick's grasp to avoid being pulled any farther.

He looked hurt by my apprehension, offended. I muttered an apology.

"I saw you during the closing prayer. You didn't even pray—you just stared at the floor."

I tried to repair the damage without appearing desperate.

"Sorry, I get nervous in crowds." I remembered my grandmother saying that about me once. Patrick stared blankly at me. Did he know it was a lie?

"Fine. See you later, I guess." He rolled his eyes, turned away, and approached another nervous-looking boy, the one who had cried at the end of the concert. Patrick gripped his wrist and shoulder. His face changed to appear tearful again as he steered the other boy up to the dwindling line of fans awaiting their moment with the traveling preacher.

I felt tears welling up in my own eyes, and I aimed my body for the front door. Brandon approached me as I made my way out of the crowd. I was afraid that he would reprimand me for not praying, or worse, try his hand at introducing me to the preacher. When he saw my face, though, he seemed to understand more than his brother had and kept a respectable distance.

"Where ya off to?"

I forget my reply, but I know it was another lie. Something about how I was only allowed out until exactly that moment, when in truth I hadn't been given a curfew. It occurred to me that I was committing one of the sins mentioned by the traveling preacher an hour before. I took it as another sign that I didn't belong, and I was surprised at my own sense of relief at the notion.

The audience had splintered off into chattering groups. No one took notice of me as I slipped out of the building into the comforting near-dark of the streetlights. Patrick glanced in my direction as I left, but he made no further attempt to speak to me or stop me from leaving. Brandon followed me out the door as I departed. He offered me a ride home in his van that had been decorated with G-rated graffiti. It looked as stylish as everything else about him, like he was being paid by some Christian shadow corporation to tell the rest of us how to be. I declined. My father was already on his way to pick me up, I said. Another lie. As soon as he went back inside I made a break for it, darting across the street and away from the little church as quickly as I could, with no clear destination in mind.

→→ ⊫✦⊨ →→

I walked along the dark side of the street in hopes of disappearing from view completely and never being seen or heard from again. Patrick had hurt me. I was not a child of God. Not faithful, not pure. There was no way I could go back into that storm of chanting, screaming, crying, promising, all for something that might not be real. My life before that night seemed so good now, so easy and untangled. I wanted it back. I regretted ever having wished for anything else.

I waited in the shadow of a pay phone for my father to come. I fought the urge to cry as I huddled behind the stall. Every car that drove by was looking for me, hoping to bring me back into the chaos of the pink church. I knew the sound of my father's truck, though, and I practically jumped into the passenger seat before he had come to a complete stop.

"How'd it go?" he asked, with a tone that said he already knew.

"It was fine." Ball in my throat. *Thank you for saving me.*

Patrick never mentioned the incident after the concert again. He resumed his usual persona in Health class like nothing had happened, joking, offering help with studies, inviting me to youth group and church services again, over and over. I lied more: a fragile, escalating stack of falsehood about a sick, perhaps dying grandmother; a family trip to the city; an extracurricular off-campus class; a disease of the mind.

I felt like a fool for wanting to be with him at all, like a gullible, sad-eyed girl in some preteen after-school special. It enraged me, and avoiding him was the only way I could think of to communicate it and still maintain my dignity. Over time he stopped talking to me altogether. By the end of the year, he had moved from the desk behind me to a desk behind another boy in the front row, his new first-period friend. I wanted to be hurt by it, but all I felt was relief.

Welcome to Adolescence:
Your Personal Survival Manual

Congratulations on reaching your teenage years. You should know straight away that the period upon which you are now embarking will be a traumatic, thrashing-in-a-tangle-of-sweat-soaked-sheets-style nightmare. Your grandmother will tell you that this is supposed to be the best time of your life but, as you already know, your grandmother is so full of shit that she should carry a mop and bucket with her everywhere she goes. It's not her fault. She's only concerned. She wonders why you are so unhappy. Polite in public yet so argumentative at home. So "dour." So "surly." So "down." A steady diet of false optimism will have that effect, you will say, and your father will scold you for being such a brat.

The truth is that the majority of the students in your school will despise you. Your friends, such as they may be, will not be able to help you; they will be too concerned with their own hopeful invisibility to aid you in maintaining yours. Please note that your only viable options for making it through this prison sentence will be hiding or temporarily blending in.

Please note that you will fail. The other boys—the real boys— are not like you. You loathe all sports. You are not attracted to girls at all. You want to be left alone. By contrast, they thrive in odiferous packs. They are hormonally charged wolves in bulky green letterman jackets, acne and hickeys in place of fur and mange, and they can smell

73

weakness. They can pinpoint your differences, your insecurities (which are considerable), and your soft and comparatively effeminate nature.

Helpful Hint #1: If everyone hates you, agree with them. Blend into the hate and thereby become one with it. Embrace how badly you suck, and perhaps your assailants will be less inclined to point it out every five minutes. Learn to despise yourself as much as you are despised. Grow to hate your face, your skin, your voice, your general presence in the world. This will at least make it easier when you have to make yourself the butt of the joke in order to keep from being harassed.

You are short and possessed of chub that never seems to go away, no matter how little you eat or how far you run (though you never try too terribly hard to change it). It embarrasses you, but then again you are embarrassed by everything. You try constantly to fold into yourself, to absorb the fat and the awkwardness into the void of your insides, if it is a void. More likely it is a collection of weird junk that no one, not even you, knows what the fuck to do with. The other boys are tall and lean and, often enough, beautiful. You will wish that at least one of them could see you in remotely the same light, but you will quickly learn better.

Try this practice exercise: Watch as the wolf pack pries open the locker of the only boy visibly gayer than you with a piece of iron rodding stolen from metal shop. Do nothing as one of them—the same one who threatened to kill your dog—pisses all over the contents, the books and papers and photos all stacked neatly at the bottom of the narrow space. Do not tell anyone afterward, not even your own family, since there is no point; neither punishment nor accountability will ever reach them. They rule the madhouse. The school staff is uncaring. For extra credit, try wondering how many of them were once wolves themselves.

Even girls, who are typically kinder, are cruel here. It will hurt more, for some reason, when they insult you, call you terrible names. It feels like more of a betrayal than when the boys say the same exact things. Not everyone is cruel, of course. Some will be funny and friendly and kindhearted. These people will offer a small amount of comfort and companionship, but it will never last and it will never be enough. Ingratiate yourself upon them, and hone your craft of self-deprecation for later and better use, but never show them the real you so that you can lose them all, eventually, growing up to be the kind of person who is great to know at a distance. People will tell you how cool and fun you are, but you will never accept it as a compliment because you know how quickly they would grow tired of your shit and leave if they were any closer.

Helpful Hint #2: Cultivate a false sense of superiority. Become a snob, even though your family has no more money or status than the majority of the other small-town Oregon kids among whom you have spent your entire life. Nonetheless, pretend that you come from a line of moneyed small-town socialites. They do not actually exist in your town—a place for the mill worker, the logger—but no one needs to know that, and no one will question you if you pretend like you aren't actually a product of the stolid American-dream-seeking middle class. Just make it convincing. Say things a bit differently, like you read in that history book, like you saw on that British television show. Say things like, "My family and I are taking a holiday together" when in fact you are spending a week on the coast that is only an hour away. Use words like *shall* and *momentous* when convenient. If you are lucky, the other kids will be deterred by the possibility of money or that you are simply *better* and therefore should not be fucked with. This will also serve you well if you get your feelings hurt, providing a safe and largely inaccessible place to which you may retreat emotionally.

You may be pleased to learn that, later in life, you will continue to feel compelled to use this faux snobbery as an easy escape in times of stress or conflict, though it will never work as well as it did when you were sixteen and terrified. You will never find the words to explain that it is a defensive tactic that you learned to survive a terrible time in your life, and the feigned superiority that you never actually felt will become a curse. (See "Welcome to Your Twenties: Compounding Your Loneliness with Unshakeable Neuroses.")

Helpful Hint #3: If Helpful Hints 1 and 2 stop working, just say fuck it and bail. Fail the eighth grade and be "required" (through familial guilt) to take summer courses to keep up. Feel absolutely nothing about it, even when your grandmother weeps softly after reading your report cards in the mail. Your subpar-at-best performance should not surprise her; you are not a good student and never have been. Still, your grandparents will react badly, like you were selling crack cocaine out of your backpack at lunch.

"You don't apply yourself," you will be told by strangers who get paid to teach you things. They will say this like they read it or heard it somewhere and believed it to be brilliant. It is not, and you know it. It barely makes sense in the context of an education system that produces graduates on a rickety assembly line for mass-market consumption, but when you say that, you will be punished for arguing. You will come to believe that most all of the school's staff were never actually young, never at any point children who struggled to understand themselves while navigating the chaos and daily horrors of a public school education. You will assume that they were born "applying themselves" and have always been successful because of it, rewarded for their hard work and diligence with ill-fitting magenta slacks and a prestigious position as the assistant librarian/guidance counselor/backup typing instructor who can now mispronounce with confidence that you, "Justin Hendrix," you are a good kid, but you just aren't applying yourself.

They will involve your mostly-absent mother, who will make a special trip down to blindside you in your happiness to see her. She will rage at you, using words like "effort" and "responsibility" as if she has any idea what they mean or any actual say in the matter from four hundred miles away. She will shout and threaten and make it infinitely worse for her lack of understanding, and you will be actively, deliberately angry about this for decades, remaining distant from her in an attempt to punish her for something she barely and inaccurately recalls. (See "Welcome to Your Thirties: Doggedly Refusing to Let Go of Past Slights.")

Over time, your unhappiness and general ability to get out of bed will approach critical mass. Your longing for people like you—literally anyone remotely like you—will override any learned survival tactics or drive to succeed (of which you have painfully little to begin with). In truth, there are plenty of people who are remarkably similar to you, but you will avoid them for fear of not seeming special. School will seem like divine punishment. Home will seem hollow, like you were never supposed to be there in the first place. You will feel infinitely older than your seventeen years, with nothing to show for it. Things that once made sense—go to school, learn the things, go to college, learn more, get job, be happy—will cease to, and it will all seem meaningless, or pointless, or both. Your future will feel like a blank page, and not one that holds the promise of good things to come. Allow this to poison your outlook for years.

The people who love you will be confused and exasperated by your behavior. Your grandmother, especially, will carry on at length, ranting at your locked bedroom door in great diatribes about how you have to "do something, anything." Blame your childhood circumstances, your lack of "real" parents, your family and childhood, all of which are certainly more fucked up than anyone else's. Tell yourself and anyone willing to listen that you have abandonment issues, even though this is horseshit, as your grandfather loves to say. You have more parents than you know what to do with. Your abandonment issues are a fiction devised to cast the illusion of depth born of hardship, of which you have faced little. You know, at least in your (rare) logical moments, that there are other kids in much worse predicaments than you. You are lucky to have been dropped into the welcoming lap of grandparents who worked hard so that you do not have to and created a lazy safe space for themselves and their children.

Survive the constant hatred from relative strangers, the threat of violence every time you walk through the doors to your first class, the annoyed-at-best teachers who look on as you suffer. At the end of the day, after all of this is past, be sure to wonder if you are a sociopath, damaged beyond repair. Finally, while this is the worst time of your life, at least take comfort from this: you will not keep any friends from high school.

An Open Grave

My friends and I had pooled our money and purchased, through some willing adult, several pints of a foul and inexpensive concoction called Mad Dog. It tasted of orange, but with a syrupy, slightly rancid flavor that my father would have defined as "cheap hooch." The terrible taste of the stuff led us to hold our noses while chugging. That way, all you could taste was the sugar until the final swallow.

We drank it and smoked whatever we had to smoke. Then they had homes to go to, other things to do, so they left. I stayed, alone, with my notebook and cigarettes, writing angsty song lyrics or one of the bleak short stories I was always working on but never finished, while the sun slowly set. Alone, in the cemetery.

It was to be expected; I was a goth kid. A foul-tempered goth kid with nothing to do. If I went home I'd just be asked annoying questions about my day, my weird hair, my white makeup and black nail polish (which was actually black felt marker), my schoolwork—none of which was ever done on time, if at all. No, the solitude of the silent dead seemed far more suitable than my family. At least until it got too cold, or too creepy, or until hunger and boredom sent me home, through the back door of my house and directly into the kitchen in search of sustenance, try as I might in those days to never eat human food.

My goth phase wasn't about being obsessed with death, though. In fact, I was very squeamish as a young person; too much delving into the gruesome realities of dying and decomposition would have turned my stomach very quickly indeed. Nor was I particularly drawn to the blended and often disturbing aesthetics, the artful carelessness, the kabuki of it all. No, as much as I wish could say I had some darkness lurking in me, in truth I fell into the scene for a much simpler and more pathetic reason: I had no friends.

It's a cruel thing, to tell a teenager that they're living the best years of their life. I heard it over and over when I was one, from strangers and family alike, and it never held a scrap of truth for me. It seems to me the perspective of a simpleton. High school tends to suck. At least for all but the lucky less-than-one-percent who, by some manner of genetic and/or social witchcraft, manage to actually thrive and seemingly enjoy their time in the public education system. I'm inclined to believe that these chosen ones are in reality just better at hiding the fact that they feel as horribly out-of-place as everyone else.

My high school was tiny. My grade and most of the others consisted of about twenty kids, an alarming number of whom wouldn't make it to the finish line, myself included. Most of the staff had worked there for just over a century—a grueling, grindingly long century from the look of it—and they were fed up with every kid before they'd even had a chance to speak or act out, as no doubt they would. I was shy and nervous, hoping not to be noticed as every day I slipped fearfully from chaotic classroom into crowded, raucous hallway, PTSD-ing my way to my locker, then into another classroom, waiting for the day to just fucking end so I could return to my bedroom and the world I loved most: my books, the little worlds I could escape into, so much better than my own.

There were fellow outcasts with whom I was acquainted, probably more out of "safety in numbers" than anything else, but none of them knew anything about my life at home, the things I was interested in and felt. My family took these for "friends," presumably because it normalized me a bit in their eyes. But my private life was very much my own. I doubt I'm special for this. Everyone has a universe all their own behind their eyes.

I was also obviously gay, something my classmates sniffed out before I did. This was the early nineties in small-town America, where homosexuality meant diseased men who stalked public areas in search of victims to convert and infect. A lot of "Fag!" and "Queer bait!" got thrown my way. Yet I told myself that no one knew, it was still my secret, and I would reveal it at the perfect and most shocking moment possible.

I had dabbled, very lightly, with sexuality and had been thoroughly repulsed by it all, so in my eyes it didn't matter anyway that I was into guys. Sex stuff was gross and uncomfortable. Being in very close proximity to someone else just felt bizarre. It exacerbated all of the things I didn't like about myself, and there were many. I entertained the idea that I wasn't attracted to anyone sexually. I entertained a sexless life, a monastic existence but with video games and loud music. So yeah, my attitude was shitty.

Something had happened to my brain starting around the tenth grade. I hated school, absolutely loathed it. I hated my own face in every mirror, my features that looked different to me almost weekly, changing before my very eyes. I silently mourned the blessed time before, in which I simply was and the chaos of teenage life wasn't clawing at me from within and without. My voice sounded foreign coming out of my own head, so I declined to speak unless I had to, giving the outside world an impression of a sulky, cantankerous malcontent—which, of course, I was.

I became, as so many high schoolers do, the beast of the house. Everyone around me feared my unpredictable rages. My parents, grandparents, and other adult relatives all adopted the same way of addressing me: a deep breath and one slow blink of the eyes, as if donning some psychological suit of armor for the onslaught of blustery, ineffectual teen rage that was likely to come at the first hint of a question, a suggestion, a reminder of any kind. My brothers and cousins would glance fearfully in my direction as I entered the room, checking my face for the look that would signal trouble. They stopped speaking to me unless I spoke first, which I didn't. I feel guilty now. At least home was stable. No one beat me (even if I deserved it sometimes). No one in my family ridiculed my mannerisms or my unusual taste in things, and no one made me go to church. Home, for all its annoyances and embarrassments, was a safe zone.

I was not a good student, or oddly stylish in the way of the "cool" outcasts. I preferred to wear shapeless, plain black clothing, the less form-fitting the better, in an attempt to make myself as invisible as possible. It hid my body, the thing that made me vulnerable, the thing that anchored me to a life I wasn't all that excited to be a part of. My grandmother, in particular, was at first perplexed, then outright irritated when I insisted on all black every time we shopped for clothes. By junior year my closet began to look like a row of shrouds, long shadows hanging ominously in the corner of my bedroom, something out of the *Addams Family* wardrobe department.

I had seen them, the kids who also wore all black like me but with more style, with precision that I lacked. Where did they get their clothes? Did they make them? I felt a kinship as they walked theatrically down the hallways of the school, eyes effortlessly forward, beautiful painted lips downturned, expression vacantly, exquisitely deathlike—but with the hint of a challenge to potential bullies. *Try it, see what happens*, those faces said.

They never spoke to me, or to anyone outside of their circle, it appeared, but I would say, "Fuck yeah" under my breath, and scurry to my next class from hell. I didn't fit anywhere, so I adopted their look and mannerisms out of a longing for companionship—the one we all have as young humans. I wanted to belong to something other than my books and my bedroom and my family, most of whom I couldn't stand. I was alone, and visibly unusual, and gay in a small, small town. I fit into the only place I found that would accept me without a complete personality overhaul.

Which is how I found myself in a cemetery, in the darkness. Night had caught up with me, quicker than I'd anticipated. As I stumbled down the little hill to the long looping road on which I'd walk home, I became aware of a change in the smell and temperature of the air ahead—cold, too cold for the lingering warmth of the evening, with the raw smell of new soil. My eyes had not yet adjusted to the lack of light in the shadows of the hill, and there was orange Mad Dog in my veins.

I slowed my pace to light a cigarette, stolen from my aunt—and saw that directly in front of me was the inky black square of a burial plot that had been freshly dug for a funeral the next morning. The hole appeared to be bottomless, an abyss. The last light of the setting sun from behind me, as I meandered through the little tombstones and old trees, was not sufficient to illuminate the bottom of it.

I'm guessing I made a hilarious sight, my frantic backward arm circles those of a Looney Tunes character on the edge of a sudden cliff. Wile E. Coyote with cheap eye makeup and scuffed red Doc Martens and a just-lit cigarette dropping from his flapping mouth. I fell backward onto the wet grass, swearing like an inexperienced sailor, before collecting myself and making my way around the hole in the ground and down at last to the road, silently grateful that no one living was around at that moment to witness what had just almost happened.

What would I have done had I fallen in? The hole, reeking of damp new earth, was at the very least six feet deep. I was, and am, five feet, seven inches tall. Had I managed to make my way back up and out—

and there would've been no guarantee of that, given my state—at best I would've been covered, absolutely covered, in mud and moisture and probably a few earthworms. I would have hobbled home, wet and filthy, humiliated and traumatized from the experience.

Even better: I fall in. I can't get out. I wait, cold and damp, until the mourners and funeral staff come the next morning. I have fallen asleep in the meantime, having surrendered to the confines of my earthen prison. I wake, blinking at the early sun, to a gaggle of strangers looking down at me as I wake: a strange boy in faux-tattered clothing and smudged eyeliner. Or I injure myself, render myself unconscious. I am found like that: facedown, unmoving. A corpse already in place, but not the one the funeral-goers had planned to put to rest that day.

They'd be outraged either way, of course. Authorities would be involved quickly. I would be hoisted out of the grave, at best with a rickety aluminum ladder obtained from the groundskeeper's shed, at worst with some kind of crane and human-sized sling, the one used to retrieve bodies from awkward places in the world. If awake, I'd be ushered into a squad car as bereaved relatives shouted at me, telling me how disrespectful I was. One of them, particularly close to the deceased, might become so tearfully distraught at my crime that her eyeliner would look just like mine after a long, cold, moist night of sleeping in a hole in the ground. The mud I acquired from sleeping in the earth would smear the hard plastic back of the police car, and the police officers would remark to each other that it wasn't even the tenth most disgusting thing to be smeared across the back of that car.

The cops would drive me home in silence, smirking one moment, disapproving the next (when they could see me looking back). I would be charged with some misdemeanor or other, and my family would be even more horrified and angry than they'd been when I was caught spray-painting profanities on an already-well-spray-painted bridge, or charged for "holding my friend's cigarette" in the park. I would be tasked with a round of community service, cleaning graffiti from the walls of the public library and the dumpster behind it, where I'd smoke cigarettes out of view as I scrubbed, angry and humiliated. Time would pass, and the whole event would be recorded in the annals of Stupid Shit Dustin Did Years Ago While Wearing Makeup. My grandmother would stifle her gasping laughter whenever she recounted it. My father and mother would both secretly tell everyone.

It would make for a better story than what really happened: I walked home, freezing, in the dark—roughly a mile of it. There were no streetlights, only the sound of geese in the fields and the occasional flash-and-fade of a passing car. I imagined myself in the beginning of a werewolf movie—the first victim, pieces of me found the following morning by a passing log truck or an old woman whose dog looked as horrified as she did—but I made it home in one piece. I pulled off my damp goth gear, showered, ate shameful human food, and slept in my bed, though I would have preferred a cave or a coffin.

Until then the cemetery had seemed like something of a safe space, where cheap booze and the darkest thoughts imaginable to a fifteen-year-old could be explored without interruption or judgment from the outside world. Two weeks before, I had deliberately cast off my virginity in the parking lot of that same cemetery, with a girl one grade ahead of me in school. She was a goth kid like me, but better at it. She wore leather jackets and long black and red velvet skirts with tears in them to school, and smoked black clove cigarettes that my lungs couldn't tolerate. The red Doc Martens I owned and wore constantly were a direct response to her suggestion that I needed a pair to "round out" my look.

It was the final test of my sexuality. I had to be absolutely certain before I started applying the word "gay" to myself, as the idiots at school had applied it to me long before I understood what they were talking about. Their role models clearly didn't have any gay friends.

I was nervous as hell, and I'm sure it showed. But it was over quickly. I mainly remember the hurried removal of clothes in the back of her parents' car, and the even more hurried pulling back on of clothes afterward.

I don't recall feeling any more or less alone afterward, but I do recall a sense of relief at having passed (or failed) the final test. I knew with certainty that I was not attracted to girls. I mean, I already knew, but that round of awkward car sex was proof enough. I had tried. I could say, with pride, that I had failed at "straight" and was something different. I still hesitated to apply the term "gay" to myself—both because it still felt damning in some "high school bully" kind of way and because it actually meant "happy" and I refused to be thought of as happy. My notebook and deliberately torn clothes were supposed to say otherwise.

We remained on friendly terms, the girl in question and I, though we never spoke of it again until a chance meeting twenty years later.

"Did I turn you gay?" she whispered, after it was agreed upon that we both remembered the events of that night, that it was okay to talk about it. She sat in my grandparents' dining room on Thanksgiving morning with her infant son drooling on her lap. Our families had known each other for longer than we'd been alive.

I almost laughed until I saw that she was serious.

"No. I blame my parents for that."

It was meant to be a joke, but she looked sad when I said it. I never told her that she was the only girl I'd ever had sex with.

Dragons

When I was twelve, I wrote a letter to Ursula K. Le Guin. I wrote it after having my mind blown wide open by *A Wizard of Earthsea*, her fantasy novel marketed toward young adults, and the voluminous, unsettlingly foreign, captivating world of problems and wonders that Le Guin had created.

In my letter I asked her (in cursive that I practiced all morning) how to start writing, where to begin. What I meant—and what I'm sure thousands of other young letter writers meant when they asked her the same question—was: "How do I write an *Earthsea* of my own?" I expressed frustration with trying to write at my age. Everything I wrote felt like it mimicked something I had already read somewhere. I felt like my life was too small to ever write anything compelling, anything of worth to someone other than myself.

She wrote me back. Her letter was brief, and typed, but signed in blue ink. It felt like I had won something. It made my week. An author had written me back. I told everyone, though no one in my family knew who she was.

"Oh, a *book* writer!" my uncle said between gulps of coffee. "I thought you meant someone from the White House. You know, a *writer*." I didn't know. I still have no idea what the hell he was talking about. It seemed strange, a crime, that no one else in my life recognized the brilliance of *Earthsea*, or had even heard of her. To me she was a big deal, as famous as Stephen King and Anne Rice and Tolkien and Ray Bradbury—the only four names I recognized at the time for being "successful" writers.

I had no idea that she was already a literary titan whose science fiction and fantasy novels crossed over from genre fiction ("if you're into that") to universal acclaim for her expansive imagination; her perfectly balanced prose, unhurried, uncluttered, unfussy; her ability to simplify and trademark concepts like the applications and pitfalls of various forms of magic, reincarnation, the afterlife, the psychology and biology of dragons.

Earthsea is the book that everyone reads at twelve and is changed forever. It changed me as an adolescent. Then, at the age of seventeen, I was destroyed once again by her Nebula Award–winning masterpiece, *The Left Hand of Darkness*. I always want to be reading that book, to live there on Gethen, the frigid alien world she created, to experience the cold, the complete absence of Earth and its genders and rigid gender roles. Eventually I would own a copy of everything she ever published, decades of lives explored, worlds constructed meticulously, societies designed and scrutinized, of oligarchies rebelled against and overthrown, of death and love and the struggle to live well and the struggle to be free. Most of them I've read more than once. Most of them I know well enough to quote verbatim, which no one has ever asked me to do.

Eventually I meet her, on a late summer evening in Portland, Oregon. It is her final appearance at Powell's City of Books, something no one in attendance has any way of knowing. She has concluded her talk on the function and craft of writing and sits behind a small table as the very long procession of gathered fans winds its way along past rows of shelves filled with books and around the back of the crowded room near the street-facing windows, like the limp tail of a lazy dragon.

She is in her late eighties now, the creator of worlds and of dragons, almost comically short behind the table a few feet in front of me, her iconic short-cropped hair gone completely white. She greets each fan politely, genuinely, but seems tired. How many of these has she done in her career? I doubt even she knows. The long dragon moves slowly forward in single file—orderly, respectfully quiet—up to the open front of the room to meet its maker. You'd think that a dragon would have no fear of an old woman, but this one does.

I try to think of something interesting to say to the woman I've admired for most of my life. Do I mention our brief correspondence? She's certain not to recall our exchanged letters from 1990. Do I make a joke? She's revered for her snark, and the talk she just gave demonstrated her gift for it amply. I'd be happy with a smile, even a tired one. Do I just mutter a demure "thank you" and flee?

She engages with each fan in such a genuine way. Look at them: so calm. They clearly spent days formulating their queries and interesting, thoughtful comments for her. They're probably all better writers than me. They probably *write daily*, and I struggle with it. My nerves are kicking me in the spine. I feel the same red rush of whatever-that-is that I felt when I had to read a short story in a high school English class, when I took my clothes off in front of another boy for the first time, when I had to stand up in a crowded morning courtroom and promise not to drink and drive ever again (I had such a hangover that morning).

Nothing I can say is worthy. I'm just going to say "thank you" and depart like a good fan. Like someone beneath the notice of a dragon should, lest they be eaten as an afterthought.

I can hear her giving advice to the excited girl in front of me. Worlds are built slowly, she says, bit by bit. Sometimes they take years to actualize, but it is important to have a solid structure already in place before you set about changing too much. It is like eavesdropping on God, and the girl sounds close to tears. I want to build a world now.

"Hello." Warm smile. A look that says she has indeed heard it all before. A sticky note bearing my name has been stuck by a bookstore employee on the front cover of *Lavinia*, the only one of her novels I have yet to read. The author opens it, signs it quickly, but waits to give it back to me. She folds her hands over the cover and looks up at me, inquisitive, like a dragon might be. My heart thumps a little.

"I wrote you a letter when I was twelve," I say. "I read *A Wizard of Earthsea* and couldn't get over it."

"Did I write you back?"

"You did. Thank you."

"I try to answer as many letters as I can," she says.

"This was a long time ago. In 1990. I asked you how to be a writer. I'm sure everyone does that." Hurry up. Dragon grows impatient, both at my back and before me.

"Well, I hope it helped you." She smiles. I did it.

"It did, thanks." Did I just lie? I haven't written a word in months.

She hands the book to me with both hands, like she knows how precious it will be to me.

"Please keep writing. We need all the help we can get," she says.

I thank her again and stumble away. The dragon crawls on. Two years later, my husband will inform me of her passing from the world.

I no longer have the letter she sent me, to my immense regret. I lost it somewhere, in the years and chaos of living that followed, but the words are still mostly with me, as if she'd typed them directly onto my hippocampus.

After thanking me for my letter, her reply to my question was three simple-enough lines: *First and foremost, a writer (of any age or level of experience) must write. They must practice and hone their craft like any craftsman must. It's hard work, but very rewarding at the end of the day.*

At twelve years old, I was hoping for something more immediate. I wanted a secret, a word of power like those in her books that would unlock the untapped literary potential hiding in my brain. I didn't want to be told the truth I already knew: that writing is writing is writing. No secret. Just hard work. Just a huge amount of "trying," a thing I did not excel at, and still don't some days.

But I took her advice; I kept writing. To be fair, I would have anyway, but in the difficult moments it helps to tell myself that Ursula K. Le Guin asked me to. Given her status in the world, and in the world within me, how could I refuse?

YOU WOULD HAVE LIKED
ME BETTER THEN

Ball and Chain

It is 1999 for a few moments longer. Soon the clock will strike midnight. The world will end. The computers will all die and we'll all be left to our own wits and wiles, adrift in a lonesome, violent world of dirty-faced bandits and burning cars. We will take to the forests and only come out at night to forage in what used to be our hometown for canned goods that we will bash open with rocks. We'll suck out the contents and cut our lips on the jagged rims. The cuts will become infected, and our once-beautiful faces will bear marks of permanent disfigurement.

I don't know how to use a gun, but I can learn. I can pick it up quickly. We can make homemade explosives from the chemicals in my dad's garage and drive a truck outfitted with rusty metal armor and spikes made of bone—functional, and of the style expected from a vehicle driven through the no-man's-land to come.

I wonder how much time we have left to prepare. Will the power shut off immediately? When will the raiding begin? Will we be safe in the city?

You and I have been on the outs for a while now. I'm so sick of waking up next to you that I get up deliberately early and relocate to the couch to finish my sleep cycle. You roll your eyes when I talk about most anything. You think I haven't noticed, but I have, and now I do it too. I used to love it when you'd play Jeff Buckley songs on your guitar, and now I want to make puke faces at the first sign of a strum. I want to mock the friends who still clap for you and drink myself oblivious.

I still love you. I tell myself those words repeatedly, though I'm just wise enough to know that I'm too young to know the first thing about love. But no one else has ever wanted to be with me like this, even if it's not really what I want. I know how pathetic I am for staying. Believe me, I know. But everyone says how good we are together. I won't let them see how untrue that is. The shame would eat me alive.

We'll be okay. We will. This collapse that's coming any minute now, it'll change us both. We'll learn new things and forget the old ones that don't matter anymore. We'll forget all of the things that make us miserable when we're together. We need each other now. I'll get good with a skinning knife, and you can hunt for food.

We can take in orphans and strays to live with us in our treehouse, our cave, the collection of city buses we've attached with flat boards and chains that will be our home. We can rename them, our children—clever names that match their scars and skills. We'll raise them to be stronger than we ever were. Form our own clan. Safety in numbers, they say, and family will never betray you. Or maybe they will. Who can say how the chaos and the violence to come will affect us? Maybe a clean break is what's needed here. It's a rebirth for everyone, everywhere.

I think sometimes—though I've never once voiced it—that you never loved me, and I never loved you, not really. I think we were the last two gays in this fucked-up town. Rarities. Lonely, like you'd expect something rare to be. All of the others like us have long since left for the city by now. We remained, and because we did it was just expected that we'd do this, partner up even though it was never a great match, or even a good one. I think we became what everyone wanted to see. I think you wish I was someone else. I wish I was too, at least when I'm with you.

It's cold on this porch, and I can tell you want to go back inside. I do too, but I stay outside, shivering as my cigarette burns down unsmoked between my fingers. The smoke tastes wrong on my tongue. Of course it does. The candy disk I swallowed over an hour ago, coated with liquid LSD, has at last begun its winding path into the avenues of my brain. I can hear my own thoughts like someone else stole my voice and is now singing them back into my skull, mocking me. They collect there, my vibrating thoughts, a dissonant pool of things I want to say but never will. You stay outside too, and as I look you in the eyes for the first time in days, I see the same strain, the same remote sadness that I know you can see in my own. You might be smiling, or maybe your mouth is moving too fast for my eyes to keep up. But you know what I want to say. We've both told ourselves that this is the right time to end it. It's a gift to both of us, really, to go out on a night of celebration like this. A way to ease the pain of it.

And then we each go to bed, alone.

And then we start our lives again, apart, on New Year's Day, a new millennium ahead.

I'm imagining the fireworks before they begin. They'll be the signal to get started, to usher us hurriedly into this new primitive world. I haven't stockpiled, but I know where to find things we'll need to survive. I've lived here my whole life, after all. I grew up outside of town, on a lonely farm. I must know something of gardening, of husbandry. The thought of killing for food turns my soul and my stomach, but I imagine our first hard winter will change that. I'll start using a bow and arrow even before out bullets have run out, and you'll be so impressed at how strong I'll become, how useful.

Our friends are calling to us from inside. Their voices are violet-tinged, syrupy to my addled brain. *Get ready*, they say, *get in here*. The final shots of the '90s are poured, and if we don't go in soon they'll be gone.

Most of them will probably not survive, but we will. We have each other, and it's more than anyone inside can say, the sad, perpetually single fools. And on nights when we're so sad at our losses we can do nothing but weep, we can turn to the other and think, "But I never lost you." It's a love story, a dark, dirty love story just waiting to happen. It's the only sliver of pure good to come from the death of the world we know.

You say nothing. You smoke and stare at the ground. I tell myself not to hold your hand, but then I do, and you give no sign that I've touched you at all. The air in my throat feels like cotton, like spun sugar, like change is coming. I'm afraid, but I'll manage.

It's 11:57. Time moves so slowly when I'm sad. Janis Joplin is singing "Kozmic Blues" through the open window, calling us in from the thin gap of light under the door. She knows something big is happening. She knows from the silence that it probably isn't good. The lyrics vibrate in the night air, and I see for a moment her apparition. Janis, in the fog across the street, her smile mischievous and wide, her pink feather boa touching the pavement, a bottle of something strong hanging loosely in her hand. She walks off into the night, into a vertical fold of time, and I wish I could go with her. *No one could, no one ever could*, she sings in her encore.

I laugh to myself, but you stay silent. *Say you want to go so I don't have to.*

We keep missing the moment, filling the space with silence. We are more alike in some ways than I'd care to admit, but it never could save us. It should be enough, or it was for a time. I'm seized momentarily by how brief that time actually was; it feels like years in this moment. I wonder how it feels for you, but I don't want you to tell me. I just want this to be done, and I'm sorry. If I regret later, I'll deal with it on my own. You don't have to help me anymore.

It's midnight now. Cheers and small explosions erupt from all around us. Everything is so loud. The sounds move through me like waves of ocean water, through my body, soaking my bones, stealing the warmth from my blood as they pass through. Children shriek from inside their homes.

The door opens to the party, to a blast of yellow and orange illumination, and we are both different people now, changed forever in the life span of an American Spirit cigarette. I wait, for a moment, in hopes that Janis might still be out there, singing, waiting. But she's not there. She's gone. One last glance into the dark. The streetlights shine brighter than they should. It could be the acid, working its slow-fast magic on my insides, or they could be saying goodbye.

Animate at last, you pull me to my feet. They feel like hard rubber blocks at the bottoms of my legs, but I'll manage. I'll have to if I plan to survive at all once the laws and police are all gone. I'll have to be on my toes, to have my wits about me all the time. I'll make it, somehow. We'll find a way to be happy.

The Married Man

Finish your cigarette. Say what goodbyes you must. Then get in the car and head south on the interstate. The drive will be long. But leaving has always come easy to you, the crackle of driveway gravel beneath tire is all it takes to close a chapter, to relegate everything before this moment to backstory. It was all pointless, like you feared it would be, but it doesn't matter now. Nothing before this moment matters.

It's Tuesday. The December day is just now creeping over the mountain ridge and onto the freeway below, a line of blue-gold light slowly consuming the horizon. Freezing air works better to sharpen your mind than the coffee or the cocaine. You have no reason to linger, staring from your front porch in one wide sweep at the life you have chosen to abandon. You made your decision weeks ago, with much enthusiasm. An exciting new prospect, an adventure. A new life in place of this one, which has become tiresome and disappointing and impossible to maintain any longer.

California awaits, a place you've only seen on television or heard about secondhand from the lucky few who have found it. Being afraid, feeling like an absolute failure—that will come later. For now, everything is either already packed into the car or given away. It's time to go.

You'll tell your new L.A. friends that you were tired of "hicks" and "hippies," which is true enough, or blame your general exhaustion with college life, or the electrical, mechanical whine inside your head, just behind your right ear, that showed up a month ago and hasn't left. A sign or perhaps a warning about changes needed. You'll grow angry and lash out at the nearby and the unsuspecting when the truth comes too near to the surface. You'll never admit that the last straw, what sent you speeding out of Oregon at sunup, was a man.

⋅—⋅ ≡✦≡ ⋅—⋅

I knew his wife. He was older than me, with children who were nearly grown, but it didn't show that much. He liked guns and cars and music that I hated, but it didn't bother me as much as it might have.

He was always friendly, and funny. His sarcastic humor was a match for my own. He was fun to be around, and good at his job. I was terrible at mine, but he never said anything about it. He picked up the slack for me at work on a number of occasions, never calling me out for being as lazy and disinterested as I knew I was. We laughed a lot together, and talked frequently about deeper things than I did with the other people I worked with. None of the others seemed as interesting or easy to talk to.

I suspected nothing out of the ordinary.

I thought we were just friends. We *were* friends, of the work variety. We had nothing and no one in common other than the people at work who knew us both, and, seemingly, a fondness for each other's company. I'd had several work friends before, genuine relationships that never went anywhere beyond the job. It's a common thing. This seemed like more of the same, until I found myself kissing him in his car.

I don't recall who initiated it, or the conversation that led up to it. Only the moment, and the *afterward*, in which (of course) a lot of things changed. I hadn't known I had felt an attraction, and I would never have guessed he did. His hand was on the back of my neck, pressing me to his mouth, and mine on his thigh, doing something similar, like we knew each other's bodies already, like it was a planned thing to make out like teenagers out past curfew in the rain, in front of my apartment, the windshield steaming, his bad music playing on the radio.

The morning after the first time we fucked was the inevitable catastrophic landslide of guilt and terror and wanting more. I was in shock; I was no stranger to men who wanted to fool around quietly, to boys who only wanted to experiment. These things are familiar to all gay men. But he wanted actual sex. Intercourse. He initiated it; that I recall for certain. I never would have, mainly out of fear of rejection, which I never could take lightly in any circumstance. I had believed that it was just a weird car kiss. I didn't think any further than that. Experience and years of emotional scar tissue told me I would be an absolute fool to expect or hope for anything else.

But then it happened, and then he was gone, and I was horrified and ashamed. I dreaded the inevitable crash-and-burn of revelation that was doubtlessly already in motion. He would be wracked with guilt once he realized what we'd done. He'd be horrified. He would break down and tell his wife. She would tell everyone, and I would be exposed as the home-wrecker I'd become, disrespectful and disparaging of the sanctity of a thing I wasn't allowed to have for myself. I would be fired from my job. I would lose all my friends once the news reached them, which it definitely would. I would never get to see him again.

It's a dirty trick the infatuated mind plays, to make me think I could have lived with all but the last thing on that list of consequences. But I did. I dreaded that one most of all.

It wasn't the first time he'd been with another man. He told me that, but he never told me anything more. I tried to get more information, to understand how someone could hide something so big from his entire existence, but the book was closed after that one admission. He never said another word about it after that first time.

He told me that he and his wife were "almost done." They hadn't had sex in over a year. They were only still married, he said, because divorce is difficult, and money matters become more complex and difficult as a result of it. I believed him then. I don't know if I do now. It seems too easy, though he never gave me cause to think that he was dishonest—well, aside from the fact that he was cheating on said wife with me. I wanted to ask him what she might do if she found out, but I was too afraid. I liked him. I liked having a secret.

I had no respect for marriage when I was younger, before I actually got married myself. My father and mother were serial monogamists; they'd been married three and four times each, respectively. With that as my template, the idea of marriage didn't hold much appeal for me. It seemed like a lengthy, expensive exercise in failure. It wasn't legal for me back then, anyway.

It didn't matter. A monogamous bond with another person? I'd never had anybody who fit the bill. My partners had been few, and far between, and fleeting. The intensity of the beginning always made the rest of the relationship feel like remainders. I never felt any of them really knew me, or wanted to, which explains why one of us always eventually left the other. By the end of my twenties I was alone and determined to remain that way.

This secret was something new. We liked each other, and we especially liked the sex we had. It made work more fun, too, to know that he was there, in the same room as me all day; that he knew this side of me that few others did and never said a word about it; the icy electric thrill of his sideways glances at me that always suggested something inappropriate. It was enough to get me out of bed on even the worst of days, when waking up on a workday in *the before* had seemed like a form of torture.

What would come of it all was a constant question in my mind, and another thing we never spoke of. He seemed disinterested in any talk of the future. I grew to feel the same after a few months, after some small fragment of awareness found its way into my consciousness, revealing the reality of our shared situation and the (un)likelihood of any actual future.

He always came over late at night or very early in the morning. I made the time, always. Beyond the sex, his presence was comforting. He always seemed happy with me, free of heavy thoughts and worldly burdens in a way that he never was at work, where people knew him, knew his wife and his family. It made me feel like his mistress, like I waited all day in black lingerie, smoking and pining, until at last he swooped in upon me and then was gone again.

I hated that comparison as soon as I thought of it, but I also found myself avoiding parties and dinners with friends in case he called. I didn't want a real boyfriend. I had no interest in dating, in finding someone without his baggage who wanted to actually be with me more than a few times a month. I didn't want that from him, but neither did I want it from anyone else. I was no longer interested in proper love.

You're not gonna tell anyone, right? That would be bad for both of us.
I'd heard it all my life.
No, I won't tell.

⊷ ⊷ ⊷

Months of this arrangement, of half wishing for something better, of terror and guilt and disgust with myself. I was enamored, and heavily in lust, for sure. It never progressed into more, and it never stopped being the only thing I really enjoyed in my life at that time. Everything else was tedium. All of our time was spent in my apartment, both of us hiding from his life behind the closed curtains of my bedroom, where the world outside ceased to matter for an hour, an evening, all the way to morning on occasion.

I could feel it transforming into something else, something unmanageable, even as I told myself that it was all fine—that no one would find out, that it was just sex and friendship, that one day it would end and neither of us would suffer for that end. We would part ways amicably, as friendly as we'd been before the night, one week after the kiss in the car, when he'd called me as I lay in my bed, asking for a moment of my time and then staying over.

I had nothing to stay for. My life was slowly blossoming into a series of failures and disappointments. The town was too small for me, boring and lonesome. Nothing was fun anymore. I had so much catch-up to do, and if love was ever to find me, it wouldn't find me there, drowning in an ocean of people I didn't want to talk to, who didn't understand me any more than I did them. I had to go eventually, one way or another. I'd known it for years. I was comfortable, but the loneliness was never too far from me, no matter how deep I tried to stuff it down. It was never far.

I didn't give him a formal goodbye when I finally decided to leave. Friends in the city beckoned, once again, and I accepted their invitation. It was easy, though it pained me to admit it. The job was easy to bail on, too, and my friends had all left for L.A. before me. I had little to stay for, except for the married man who asked to stay over twice a month, the married man who kissed me like he would never kiss anyone ever again, every time, who looked at me like I was an incomprehensibly foreign thing when I talked about the books I loved and ancient history and existentialism, never giving up too much of himself while always listening intently, wide brown eyes trained on me like mine was the only voice he'd ever heard. Those conversations had seemed so powerful and important as they happened, as I teased out his loves and hates—those he'd allow me, at least—amidst my own.

He found out I was moving out of state from a mutual coworker. I couldn't find a way to tell him that didn't feel like a betrayal, so I simply didn't. I let him find out through our shared work people. Cowardly of me, I know. And also strategic of me, in retrospect, to give myself no obstacles until after the deed was already done. But mostly just cowardly.

He stopped calling, and I stopped hoping he would. I stopped preparing my closure speech, my explanation for choosing to go away. It was flimsy, anyway. It lacked a compelling premise. "I want more than this." That was all I could think to say. Would he have understood, had the conversation ever taken place?

We just stopped, like we had never happened, like his secret words to me in the darkness of my apartment had never been spoken. He seemed remote at work, but encouraging, supportive in a distant way. It was a relief, in a way, that he appeared to accept my departure so easily. It also made me paranoid, like he was hiding his real feelings about it, waiting for the right moment to let them loose—angry, wounded emotions that would make the process of leaving even more difficult than it already was.

Maybe he had expected it. Whatever his real thoughts on the matter might have been, he never shared them with me. He didn't even ask where I was going. We carried on like friendly-if-distant coworkers until the day I left. He never asked me for anything more.

Would he miss me? Had I broken his heart in secret? He never gave me any clue as to how he really felt. He just moved on, or away, or back into whatever his life was like without me or before me. How many other men did he do this with? I have wondered ever since. I have wondered if I was the only one. It seems unlikely. Maybe he was the smart one, to just revert back to whatever he'd been before, once he knew I was departing. Maybe he had other secrets in his life to take my place. A piece of me hopes he did. Another piece hopes I was the only one.

I wasn't in love, not exactly. I knew just enough to avoid that pitfall. I was old enough not to dive in headfirst, as I might have if I'd been younger; I'd already had a few relationships, however doomed at the start, explode in my face. I knew it was okay to let go. I knew it was okay to hope for more with someone else, even if I didn't necessarily want it with anyone else. I knew on some level that I would never have what I really wanted with him—a life with someone, a piece of the happiness I saw all around me and envied. Even if it was a lie, even if it was an illusion, I envied it.

I sometimes wonder if it might have been easier if I hadn't. It would have made the end of the thing less confusing. It would have made for a simpler break if I could have just used "love gone wrong" as my fuel for departing. It burns cleaner, more efficiently than the wet tangle of lust and pride and shame and regret that I carried with me out of town. I wrote him a goodbye letter and then destroyed it in the fireplace. I left at dawn, my entire life crammed into a moving truck as snow fell to cover my tracks.

No real goodbye. No drawn-out explanations or confessions. No need to say *I'm sorry*, to say *I wanted more*, to say that I would have stayed if he'd asked me to. Not exactly love. More like the anticipation of it. More like a placeholder that could have been love, or should have been, in a better world.

The world changes as soon as the car crosses the border from Oregon into California. The road itself is different; the lines of white and yellow paint on the asphalt are more recent, the cracks and potholes, though there are more of them, are filled neatly with shiny black matter that looks like obsidian from the blurred perspective of your car window. The trees here seem to group themselves together in different patterns. There's more sun, and it shines at a peculiar angle here, a better angle for sunlight to shine at. It seems higher in the sky now, more self-aware. A star masquerading as a sun, guiding you south and away.

The Anxious Monologue
of How I Got Married

It's my third vodka tonic. I'm waiting for my husband to come home. He works later than I do, and when he gets home he's tired. I'm tired too, but I stay up later than I should so I can spend time with him. Sometimes I don't want to, and sometimes I don't want to have sex, but I do it anyway because he wants to and it's not his fault I'm so closed off; he probably didn't know that about me when we were just dating. He wants sex more than I do, and it makes me feel guilty, and it makes me feel just old.

I *am* old, at least compared to him. I married a younger man and I'm insecure about it. I'll be the first one to visibly age, or perhaps I already am. Each glance in the mirror these days makes me cringe and turn away, though I still look comparatively good for my age. It was only a few years ago that I thought I was in my prime, a late bloomer but a good one. Now I look like I drink a lot, because I do.

He doesn't care. He sees something I don't, or can't. I'm afraid it's some kind of elaborate lie and that he's secretly disgusted by the sight of me.

Left to my own devices, I'd probably drink less, or at least that's what I tell myself. Then I'd weigh less, since I happen to know it's all booze weight even though we cook with the fervor of mad scientists on the verge of a breakthrough, and I always indulge. I come from a long line of hedonists. Addictions and low willpower are common with us, and resolve always takes a back seat to the moment.

On my own I'd eat mostly vegetarian. I'd sleep in more, be social if I felt like it, fuck whoever I want—empty, lonely sex but just as satisfying in the moment. I'd read more books and watch less television and be constantly, constantly physically active like the people I see in their shiny form-fitting exercise gear, running down the street like their pretty, fulfilling lives depend on it while I sit in my car at another red light, on my way somewhere to sit some more.

He drinks more than I do. I worry that I married an alcoholic. Not that I would have said no. My prospects have always been few—other gay guys don't like me much. They think I'm offensive; not at all funny, too weird, too goofy, too emotionally inaccessible to date. They're probably right, but my husband doesn't think these things about me, it seems.

He's home now: sticky and ruddy and tired-eyed from working in the sun all day.

"Honey, we might have to go to the roller-coaster park while we're in Milwaukee. I miss it," he says as he pours us vodka shots. I already have an almost-full drink sweating down to the coaster on the coffee table, but it doesn't matter.

We're going to Wisconsin in September to get married again, in front of his family and his lifelong friends, even though we were married in our kitchen last May. I'm not nervous, I claim, but I imagine they are, if only to bolster my own confidence a bit. Their only son moved to the big city and found himself a husband. They'll be so disappointed when I show up and I'm all average looking and plain spoken with weird eyebrows. They'll wonder what falsehoods I invented to trick him into marrying me when he's the thin one, the one with the cool career, the one with the tattoos and piercings, the born extrovert.

I have nothing inscribed on my skin. If I am in a self-loathing mood, feeling that my youth is past, it looks especially unremarkable to me, a blank canvas of time already spent. A long time ago I was fat. I lost it, through panic and worry more than anything else. (Hollywood diet secret! Take note.) I've gained some of it back, mostly by trying to be the fun boyfriend. Apparently it worked, since now I'm the fun husband. But I'm also the heavier of us, and it kills me every day. It's not his problem, but he gets to share the benefits: my obvious discomfort in my own skin, my inability to stand crowds for long, my fear of any perceived spotlight. It's actually kind of shocking that I left my apartment long enough to meet him.

It was ultimately the heat that drove me out.

I'd trudged through three tedious jobs and four messy, unrecoverable living situations before being deposited via U-Haul and now-absent friends onto the sad end of Stark Street in a stuffy, sweltering one-bedroom death trap so miserably hot it must have been built directly above the entrance to hell. Even the cat thought so. He would stare at me, lifeless on kitchen tiles, unblinking eyes imploring me to flee, to save myself. I would stay, though, and our only reprieve from the heat would be the cool bath water we'd sit in, contemplating the hopelessness of our situations.

Yeah, I took baths with my cat. Say something.

The apartment had seemed like a score—a place to retreat and mourn the loss of the only good thing to come my way since uprooting and leaving the life I knew. I was single again, painfully so. The partner I'd placed so much faith in, invested so much of my own happiness in, had turned out to be a master of feigned sincerity and the ol' secret life— the humiliating calling card of all relationships thus far in my life. He had been cheating on me, not with another person, exactly, but with all of them, with *everyone*, by way of a gay hookup app.

I could have dealt with it if he'd wanted to fuck other people, or if he was simply tired of the us that had evolved in our six months together. But even when confronted with evidence, his chosen method of defense was more lies, and when that failed, a twisted path of rhetoric that avoided the issue in favor of blaming me for finding out, for "squeezing too hard."

Of course, I remember thinking. *That's how dishonesty works.*

There had been no drawn-out goodbye, just a single brief and venomous exchange. It could have been a clean break if I hadn't been so completely blindsided by it, so hurt. Instead, I was left with an open, jagged wound that stung and seeped as my most-of-me labored feverishly, day and night, to correct itself, to pull itself back into position. So far, unsuccessfully.

He had been my favorite thing, my hard-earned prize. Then, in the span of a day, he was the worst decision I'd ever made. And even knowing that, my loneliness betrayed me. I would have taken him back. I still would've tried to fix it. My weakness was a toxin that my system refused to clear. I was a fool, and a spineless one at that. The shame of my own reaction was unbearable.

I had resolved, angrily and as loudly as I could broadcast it, to remain alone for the rest of my life, like we all do after a relationship crashes and burns. I would learn to love myself. I would only ever love my cat—the only man who'd ever be good enough, the only one who'd never betray me. I would feel nothing ever again, just drink and fuck the pain away and never care for anyone. I'd become one of those cool, hard-drinking, chain-smoking perpetual bachelors who make everything seem so easy and simple. I was done with love, with wanting to be with someone, with yearning for a like-minded companion.

When the message came—on a Friday afternoon, almost as if on cue as I limped into my apartment after a brutal ten-hour shift—I immediately dismissed it.

"Let me know if you want to grab a drink sometime."

A single, succinct line. No greeting, no wit, or clever pitch with which to rope me in. Not that it would have had the intended effect. I was burnt; bitter and lonely and pissed off at everything. My life was a perfect trash fire. All the secret regrets, old fears that I thought I had dealt with, moments of guilt and shame held over from past versions of myself—everything I'd been staving off from years and decades prior, things I had never been brave enough or alone enough to face—it had all been waiting for the perfect moment to strike. That time was now, as I languished and sulked in my new apartment that I couldn't find the strength to organize or decorate. My living room was an undulating ocean of half-empty boxes and stacks of books, piles of clothes and randomly placed bits of furniture—the standard potential red flags of the compulsive hoarder.

The dating app had gone largely unnoticed, having been installed months prior on my phone by an ever-concerned sister-in-law amid a red wine haze and overabundant Christmas decorations.

"You need a boyfriend. You're fun! You're too well adjusted to be single."

"I am not well adjusted," I told her. "I have a Xanax prescription literally for this visit." And fun? I was so sick of myself that I avoided my own reflection. The sound of my own voice was grating.

I never used the app for anything other than being an invisible creep, watching without being noticed. There's something transfixing, hypnotic indeed about observing, imagining the lives of strangers as they pass you by. I've always been a people watcher, and if anything in the modern world feeds that beast, it's a thing on your phone that allows you to watch as people try to be desirable. I had a profile, but it was unimpressive to say the least, a single photo taken at a good angle and some drivel about how I'm probably too busy to date.

I already had Friday plans. They involved a great deal of sweating and sulking. Also writing things I hated. I was tired of writing, though it was one of the only things that made me feel better—odd since I could rarely stand the sight of my own words after they'd left my brain. I considered calling a friend, but everyone was either busy or unbearable.

But this guy on the app, this clearly misguided weirdo, maybe he wasn't unbearable. He had a lot of tattoos, though. And he was thinner than me, a set-in-stone deal breaker. He smiled in his photos, something I resolved early in life to never, ever do. He seemed generally … happy?

It's one drink, said Optimism. *If it doesn't work out (and it won't), you can come back here and be resentful and solitary like it never happened.*

He's young, Pragmatism countered. *Way younger than you. You've made that mistake before, and now you're alone, dying of heat stroke. Stick to people your own age.*

You're a Libra! You can get along with anyone! Optimism said, quoting the big astrology book resting in the corner of my living room, propping up lamp parts I have yet to reassemble. *Besides, you are simply too old to be this bitter. It's unattractive. Be happy.*

We don't owe anyone anything, Pragmatic Me snarled in response. *Can we start drinking yet?*

I couldn't decide which part of myself I was more sick of.

Fine, one drink. A single line back was all I would give this situation. A casual, easy response. One that belies my horror at the thought of dating ever again.

"How's tonight for you?"

"Great. Where should we meet?" He replied almost immediately. Odd. Potentially alarming.

"Do you want divey or upscale?"

"Divey, for sure."

Very well, younger tattooed stranger. You've passed one test. But there shall be more! Upscale seemed like too much work. I was in no mood for the empty, overly glossy cheer of an upscale establishment. I wanted strong drinks from a bartender as guarded and surly as I felt.

I told him to meet me at Thatchers, the intimidatingly loud dive bar just up the street from my apartment that I'd been too afraid to enter before. A dick move, perhaps. I could have taken public transit to anywhere in the city instead of having him trudge all the way out to me.

I stepped out of my airless apartment and into a summer windstorm that seemed to descend upon the street in response to my decision. Hot wind pushed at me. I bowed my head and leaned into it as I walked—determined, suddenly, to get out of my own miserable head, if only for an hour or two. I was wearing shoes I had paid too much for at Hollywood Vintage for a Halloween costume and decided to add to the general wardrobe. They clacked awkwardly on the sidewalk.

As I walked, I prepared my conversation points, my hopefully clever inquiries, my exit strategies—both the nonemergent and "get out now" versions. I had taken no more than a dozen steps when an unfortunate bicyclist landed, head over handlebars, squarely on her back in the middle of the street.

There was no traffic yet, thankfully, but I was already running late by way of indecision over whether I should actually go through with this, and then from carefully choosing which of my black shirts to wear with the black pants I'd already selected. They all looked alike, but I could see the difference.

Healthcare-professional me said "Stop" and "Help." Late-for-what-might-be-a-date me said "Fuck" and "Great."

I stopped. I helped. She would live, it seemed, and the people who'd just parked their car in the street with flashers on were, miraculously, trained paramedics. I was not, because I knew what paramedics saw in their line of work, and I could never drink that much gruesome away. But no matter; they had arrived like Subaru-driving angels, better help than I could ever be. Yet again, I had been spared the fate of actually having to use the Basic Life Support techniques I was required to learn at work.

Just go. Stop being late for everything, Pragmatism and Optimism said, in rare unison.

Yeah, I'm going.

He was already there, and in the not-so-far-off future I would know him to be chronically punctual. He had silver hair in the style of the Portland hipster, which I incorrectly assumed was artificial. He was tall and lean, pierced and tattooed in a way that said "unavailable" to me. I was plain and weird and immediately felt awkward, like I always do in a crowd. Like Wednesday Addams in a disco. The air was nice and cool, though, and there was vodka eyeing me from the shelf behind the bar.

You can do this, Optimism says, in the encouraging tone of my grandmother as I waited for the bus on my first day of first grade. I felt about the same that day.

It's just drinking and talking, after all. Things at which you excel.
He doesn't seem disgusted. He's...friendly.

"A game of pool?" His smile was oddly charming, oddly mischievous, a wolf pup at playtime. He had the clear blue eyes I always wished for as a child.

I can't play for shit, but sure. He won, easily. He laughed at my bad jokes. His hair was naturally that color, which no one ever believed. He was a farm kid like me, displaced by the same life circumstances as my own, hungry for something other than the life he knew. I felt somehow overdressed in the face of the effortless homeless-chic style he wore so well, though I was wearing what I always did. He smiled when I made fun of the hillbillies who played Shania Twain on the jukebox. I smiled back—the good smile, too. The one I used when I wanted it to be noticed.

Not so bad, is he?

Just wait. Drinking makes people honest. He'll drop some flaw soon enough.

I ordered more drinks, against my better judgment. A lot more drinks. He was funny, and that astrology book was right, at least about one thing. We talked films, which he helped make for a living. We talked about coming out to our families, both oddly lucky in that. We talked about small towns and how suffocating they were. We talked about dating, and how terrible we both were at it.

We talked video games. I mentioned that I had some in my apartment, conveniently just down the street.

"You have the new *Mortal Kombat*? Let's go."

"To my place?" I was unprepared for this. My place was a sloppy, cluttered nightmare.

"Yeah, can we?"

What have you done, slut? Pessimism is a booming, paternal voice of disapproval.

Also: *Mortal Kombat? Are you twelve?*

He was great at pool, but no match for me at murder games. The apartment was still ridiculously hot, even at that hour, but the vodka from the bar and the wine we had picked up on the way home made it bearable. I was too drunk to care anymore about how mismatched we may or may not have been. My cat sat on the edge of the sofa, happily perplexed by the visitor, less standoffish than with most. Call it superstition (or "cat lady wisdom"), but my cat was my barometer for gauging the moral worth of any person who stepped through my door. If he was wary, so was I.

He was not.

We talked exes: shitty, emotionally extortive exes. He had a few too (who doesn't?), but he didn't look half as wounded as I felt all the time. I found myself wishing that I could have known him before all of this life-trauma had landed on me, crushed me down into this jaded, suspicious thing I'd become.

You would have liked me better then.

The evening ended too quickly, for a much-needed change. He didn't stay over, though I would've let him. One-night stands weren't really my thing, but it beat whatever I had planned before he messaged me.

Oh well. It was a good evening. Optimistic Me at last agreed.

Even if you'll never hear from him again, Pragmatic Me replied. *Is there any aspirin in this dump?*

<hr />

"Did you really just write a story about us?" he asks.

"It's more about me, but yeah."

He's sitting on the couch in his underwear. He's so uninhibited I want to scream. I never will be—and I never was—and I don't know how I can explain that to my almost-and-often-naked husband who has always been perfectly, obnoxiously lean and never gives it a second thought. He doesn't seem to care at all that our relationship might have been attained by way of me sacrificing my resolve to be perfect. *I should run endlessly*, I tell myself silently. *I should do yoga until I can contort myself into a human pretzel, horrifying but accomplished.*

I can't. I can't. I'm too busy, and that's what I'll always tell myself. I get tired more easily than I used to. He's early thirties, still in possession of some fragment of youth that keeps him going no matter how overworked, no matter how exhausted, no matter how little sleep we allow ourselves. I'm so close up to forty that I want to die whenever I think about it. I want to die in a crystalline tornado of cocaine and martinis and all of the other unhealthy shit I was still filling myself with when I was impervious to life and time like he still is. It's maddening, and I know how irrational I sound when I bring it up, so I mostly don't anymore. He doesn't notice, anyway. He just smiles and kisses me like I'm *not* teetering on the verge of decrepitude, like he sees the oh-so-young me who he never actually met.

He texts me every day to tell me how much he loves me. I always text back right away, but the truth is that I don't know how to love like he does. I'm afraid I'm a liar. I'm afraid that I tricked this person who obviously has some sort of void inside into filling *my* void because I was afraid of starting the process in which someone finds a way to die. I was hungry for something new, something to distract me from myself, and it came, at last, in the form of him, this obvious madman who loves me more than I could ever love myself.

I did what I had to in order to keep him. I didn't want to be found someday in my sad one-bedroom apartment, dead for weeks, unused champagne glasses gathering dust on the kitchen shelf where they'd been placed and had never moved since; placed lovingly, optimistically, in days where there'd been more hope and something to look forward to. I'd rather be someone who let himself go for the right reasons. I'd rather be a liar.

"Can I read it? Your story about us."

"No. It isn't finished," I lie, but sweetly.

0 December

There are holes in the door, two holes that you put there with your now-bloodied fist so the air of our bedroom mixes with that of the rest of the apartment. Through them, you shout to me all of the reasons why I am unsuitable as a spouse, though you are the one lying in our bed at four thirty on a Sunday afternoon drinking wine from a box on your nightstand, direct from the spigot.

It is the second day of this behavior, this barrage of things you "couldn't tell me" until you were soundly manic and soundly day-drunk and enraged at my lack of response and my lack of willingness to fight with you in your sad, self-constructed arena.

This month is your kryptonite, your annual dreaded Waterloo. Something takes you over every year at this time, in December when your work slows down, though you never seem prepared for it. The weather slows too, and the cold keeps us indoors where, predictably, you fall apart once again like something is actually wrong, but nothing is. Christmas is four days away.

I have dialed 911 out on the keypad of my phone. I have only to hit the green oval marked "call" and the police will come. They will arrest you, citing willful destruction of property and intent to self-harm. I don't want to, I say, but in truth I do, if only to spite you and so I can sleep for a while and decide whether this increasingly tiresome and embarrassing arrangement of ours is worth salvaging.

Smart people don't have to deal with embarrassing shit like this, I think. They don't have husbands who drink too much. They are strong and would have long ago told you to deal with your obvious addiction or get the fuck out. They don't linger like I have. They don't wait around for you to maybe get better someday. They bail. They value themselves enough to bail, like my mother says I should, like your own best friend says I should. This is a pattern, he says. A cycle for you. A long-standing one that predates our relationship and has always and only ever ended badly before, in his experience, with cops being summoned and handcuffs put to use and volleys of rage-infused words screamed in the street.

You won't be screaming in the street at me, I say. I'll deal with this here and now. I'll let you sober up in jail, and you can sign your fucking divorce papers there too, I say, in a quick-fading match-strike of anger and fist-clenched fortitude.

But will you actually do it? The fire dies once more to a glow, to a despondent ash. *Can you follow through?*

It's not anger that I feel, not exactly, not exclusively. It's something deeper and sloppier and more difficult to navigate. Or maybe it's just anger, but it borders on numbness, on cruel and unrecoverable apathy. It frightens me. I know well enough what the opposite of love is: not rage and not spite. It is something colder and more vacuous. It is the lack of those things—the void, the emptiness of space, a simple nothing where once there was a twisting clot of emotions to pluck from and use as needed, to fuel the partnership into which I entered without a second thought. How foolish. How desperate of me.

◄━ ⵣ◆ⵣ ━►

A square of white and purple Christmas lights blinks to life on the porch across the street from my car that I've driven five blocks down and parked behind a low-hanging tree so that you can't find me. The tree inside the house follows them, winking in full spectrum at me from the front window. My phone's screen winks back from the empty passenger seat as you call me again, but I don't answer, again. Here we are.

This one is much worse than before. This is permanent damage, or at least that's how it feels for me right now. I can never let it go. It's not in my nature to do so. And if, by some weak miracle, we remain together after this horror show has played out, I will never fully forgive you for this breach, this betrayal that I should've expected and avoided, even if I say I have.

My phone vibrates nonstop from where I've laid it in the passenger seat as you call and text incessantly, alternating insults and barbs with pleas for me to come home and "work it all out," which I did three times already today to no avail.

I won't come back again. I'll freeze to death in this car if I have to. I'll call out sick and block your number. I'll find a lawyer and have a restraining order placed. I'll bring armed policemen into the house with me to collect my things as I depart for my new life alone, again. Alone again.

I am not your frail wife. If we married for love, you have poisoned it now, I say. You have ruined the love, and I don't want it anymore. I just want to sleep in the bed by myself.

I'd kill for a drink. A stiff vodka tonic. That's what we drank on our first date, and it's what caused this mess, and I'm a hypocrite for wanting it. But I understand why you do it, even if I pretend like I don't. A just-dirty-enough martini, with a twist or an olive or with nothing at all. I don't care. A shot of tequila. Fuck sipping it. Down the hatch, all at once. Express lane to my central nervous system. Make this nightmare bearable. Or a whiskey, almost neat. One ice cube that my father would scoff at, dropped in with defiance. I don't even like whiskey, but I want it anyway.

I get why you do it. Anything to take the edge off.

━━ ◆ ━━

Everything was fine, and still is in a way. No external trauma came to our door to infect you. No real event sparked this, other than the slowness and me asking you to not drink wine for breakfast, and not for lunch, and to not drink vodka with dinner (or for it). Now you tell me I'm horrible and you send me photos of your self-inflicted wounds over text and then say, "Don't threaten me" when I promise to call the cops if you don't stop. Three photos, a gridlike pattern of scratches. Shallow cuts on your arm, designed to harm me, not you, and it works. It's shockingly childish and evil of you, and it works just as intended. I'd rather see them on myself.

I stare at the photos until I can't anymore, until they've been replaced, overlapped with more poorly constructed messages about how all of this is my doing. The scratches on your arm, your stupid meltdown, our problems as a couple in general are all because I "don't listen" and because I'm "hard to be around."

I don't drink my breakfast, you fucking baby, I say silently. I should say it to you instead of to the stagnant air in my car, but I fear making you react worse than you already have.

Weak. And hopeless. Not you this time, but me. How blindly stupid of me to think that you were as upstanding and stable as I had believed. It's always like that when you don't know someone and you want them to love you. Rose-tinted glasses, large and heart-shaped, and uncaring of the bad end, the sad and treacherous path they lead us all down.

The phone has stopped buzzing now. My text messenger app has gone silent, the screen dark, so no longer am I fickle, no longer am I a faithless piece of shit who's always had one foot out the door. No longer do I need to just come home and crawl in bed with you and make it all better with only my presence and willingness to pretend like the last two days haven't scarred me and corrupted my view of you forever.

Did you jump out the window and onto the street below? Did your Malbec-soaked organs fail you at last?

Stop. "Stop that," I say out loud. The words fog the air that is trapped with me in my car. *You would die if he did. You would throw yourself out that same broken window and land on the pavement right next to him and you know it.*

I'm ashamed, but the car is freezing, and the lack of light from my phone is frightening. I'm one of them: the people I mocked and looked down upon. The wife whose husband cheats and slaps her around when she says something, but then he cries and says sorry and that's that and everything is just fine again. The child whose mother puts his hand to the burner in a fit of rage. His hand is bandaged and his fingers don't bend now, and all he wants as the nurse winds the gauze around his arm is his mother. The dog, kicked and ejected out onto the porch. Kick me again if you must, Dog says. Just let me back inside.

I am among you now, the dejected enablers, the willing abused. I am a low-ranking member of your party, the one I believed myself better than and stronger than and set apart from by way of my intelligence, which is barely above average at best, as this weekend and my inability to deal with you has proven.

I created this beast. Or fed it, at least. I wanted you to love me. We were having fun.

Snow is near to falling. Low clouds roll over the city with the promise of it, fat gray frogs full to bursting with it. You will have to make a decision soon, and so will I.

But mine is made already, try as I might to deny it. I won't give up yet, on you or on "us." I'm too entrenched in our life together. I'm too in love with the idea of you. It feels like such terrible, humiliating weakness now, like the kind of compromise someone makes when they have nothing else and nowhere to go.

I won't give up. I knew it when all of this started, I suppose. Admitting it makes this entire horrible production seem shamefully pointless. Now you've gone silent and, like terrible clockwork, I worry and fret. Phone stays dark. My mother waits for an update, to know that I'm okay, but I have nothing to tell her. I regret ever telling her about this at all, now. I knew how it would end. It explains why I was so angry. I knew I'd let this go, at least on the surface. I knew I'd file it away, keep it for ammunition in later arguments, like a petty, vengeful child.

Phone stays dark. What are you doing? The silence says something far worse than the endless phone calls and text message screaming.

Do not pick up that phone, you weakling, you simpleton, my head says, and I don't. Not yet.

I signed the paper. I signed it before you did. We legally agreed to be happy together. Our dearest friends saw us do it. But I won't say, "In sickness and in health," not even in my mind. It's too clichéd and too stupid, and also too true, and the thought of compromising at all makes me want to make holes of my own in the dashboard, in the windshield that keeps me only somewhat cold instead of hypothermic.

If I leave—if I really leave—I won't come back. It's too sad to consider. *Please get better, please fix yourself so that things can be better, don't leave me alone*, a child begs somewhere inside me, and I'm enraged again, but the cold air and the twinkle of Christmas lights quells the rage, and I'm just sad again, and incredibly lonely at five blocks away.

It's not your fault that I'm like this. It's not your fault that I hid so much of myself from you at the beginning. It's not your fault that I'm always waiting to be left, that I expect it from everyone inherently.

First flakes of snow on windshield. More lights on houses and in them. A blow-up snowman in a fenced yard waves at me and I look away quickly, try not to acknowledge him as I get out of the car and head back, back to our apartment, back upstairs to where you were when I left, to pick up the pieces and move on or start over or whatever other people, normal people, do.

The houses seem so warm as I walk down the street, peering in as the cold numbs my toes, burns my face. The people inside seem so happy. It's an illusion, I tell myself. They have problems just like me. Christmas is coming to life all around me. Stop, wait. Let me deal with this first.

THE END

National Rhubarb Pie Day

Summer. We are just off the Oregon coast, heading out to open sea in a bowrider. The sun is shining. Gulls and cormorants follow us in lazy, effortless circles overhead, black and white triangles framed in gray-blue. The forward-up-down motion of the boat feels gentle, welcoming, and the water seems not to move at all, like we are skating over a solid, frictionless surface, escaping the chaos of land for a simpler place where there are only birds and cloudless sky and the shimmering expanse below us. The air, tinged with salt and seaweed, swirls around us and over us.

The ocean is a mirror, one that a person could pass through into an upside-down world in which everyone walks and talks in reverse. The ocean birds, now underneath, fly in backwards circles against the air currents that keep them aloft. The reverse-trees grow down, their roots tangling, unseen in the earth, with roots from the upright trees in my world, a network of twisted underground anchors holding both worlds together.

I daydream of the mirror world with no care for the fishing trip itself, though I was the first one to be excited this morning as everyone woke. I want a glimpse of the backwards birds, the upside-down beachgoers basking in the sun. Too enticing an invention to not be real. I reach out, stretching across boat rim and open water to grasp the metal tie bar that curves its way around the rear edge of the boat. It appears to have been made for me to grasp. The water seems luminous.

I have already been asked more than once not to lean on the edge while the bowrider is moving, but I am five and not very good at following instructions. I know not to do it, but I ignore my grandmother's repeated warnings. Her voice breaks through the wind in my ears—harsh now, metallic sounding. I know I'll be scolded. One more moment. A little look.

As if in response, as if to teach me a hard lesson in obedience, in caution, the boat and the ocean seem to lurch in unison. My grip falters, and time either hastens or slows. My own weight, displaced by the speed of the boat, is sufficient to push me through the open space—just wide enough for my small body—between the edge of the boat and the metal bar, and into the shining water. A chorus of alarm from my family members aboard is the last sound to reach me before I break through, into what I now fervently hope is the mirror world I envisioned.

<hr/>

Winter. The morning air was foggy, close to freezing. Southern Oregon has an almost desert-like climate: dry, scorching summers, and frigid winters that last well into March and April some years. Visibility was decidedly low, but I knew the way—far better than I wanted to—and there was rarely another moving car to be seen at that time of morning, not until I reached the main road that connected my little neighborhood with the rest of the city. The hospital was south, situated on an elevated hilltop ridge that gave it a foreboding appearance, looming down as you drove past on the I-5. Before I worked there I would see it and imagine dark horror movie things taking place there.

I had volunteered for the early shift not because I was a morning person but because starting work at a painful five o'clock every weekday meant that my brain didn't really have to wake up until later. Most of the healthcare staff wouldn't arrive until well into my shift, and the patients were still sleeping. The hospital was a veritable ghost town for me to wander sleepy-eyed, often hung over, seething inwardly at my own inability to make what the professionals call "positive life choices."

I hated my job, vehemently hated everything about it. I was a materials technician, a fancy way of saying I delivered medical supplies from the warehouse to various departments. It's one of those weird hospital jobs that no one knows about until you get hired as one. Every morning I woke up miserable, resentful, wondering with aching brain and gritted teeth why, in college—a standard state university with standard, average everything, as far as I could determine—I chose to major in English and Literature.

The head of the department was also the poetry instructor. I remember her handing me back a story, the paper clip I'd used to fasten the pages together removed and replaced with a vertical staple. There were no marks on the pages, no corrections or suggestions other than her name and the date on which I had submitted it, five days prior.

"I find the prose to be a bit heavy-handed. A bit choppy."

She wore brightly colored dresses and shoes with sunflowers and tulips on them. Her blonde hair was long and flawless. Her lipstick and jewelry always matched her dress and shoes. Her expression was always some version of a smile—teeth touching, eyes held benevolent and wise in what should have been bemusement and interest, but often enough her smile would sink into a kind of exasperated grimace when one of her students ran long in their attempts at conversation in or after class.

"Your prose might benefit from learning more about poetry. They're a lot more interconnected than people think."

She held out her hand flat, palm up, in my direction, either to denote the people in the statement as specifically me or as a way of physically gifting me with the knowledge in her statement. Her nail polish matched her eyeshadow.

She had a framed poster on the wall of her office that sported the quote, "Poetry is to prose as dancing is to walking" with old-timey feather quill pens on one side and a sunflower on fire on the other.

"Have you considered taking one of my poetry modules? There are several."

She'd been published, in periodicals and anthologies, I was told. I never knew which ones and I never read anything she wrote, though I heard plenty of her poetry in class (the class was not about poetry).

"I don't really like poetry enough to take an entire class on it," I told her, and I could almost feel the room darken as her mood did the same.

"A lot of people want to write, but it really is about putting the work in, and about paying your dues to the art first."

Now it seemed like a useless degree I never used for anything other than to correct my friends' spelling and grammar. Still, that morning I had arisen to a surprising and rare upsurge of personal optimism, which was why I had considered skipping out on work in favor of a day spent in bed, writing notes and researching what would hopefully, this time, be that first novel, or at the very least a short story of publishable quality.

I had enough sick time left in my bank for one more absence before disciplinary action was taken. Hating one's job creates a need for many,

many sick days, during zero of which I had actually been ill or otherwise incapable of working. But I knew how they'd react, my coworkers. "Absent *again*," they'd say with a roll of the eyes and a manufactured tone of annoyance as they checked my inbox for tasks they'd have to cover now.

They were as sick of my shit as I was, and I didn't blame them. My complete lack of investment in the job showed in my performance, in my lack of consistency, and in the dead-eyed expression I wore every day in that place. I imagine I looked like an absolute mess of a person. A drug addict, perhaps, or a serial murderer in the making. Still, that was probably better than whatever judgment I'd face if I discussed my dream of a writing career with anyone there: most likely the passively caustic "Oh, that's cool," followed by a great deal of ridicule after I'd left the room.

So I dragged myself, as always, from house to freezing car. I shivered and swore, but the automatic coffeepot had delivered; there was caffeine en route to my bloodstream. By the time I would see the hospital, I would at least be functional, if not friendly.

<hr />

I am a child, too young to think that a simple tumble into sunlit water could spell death for me, or for anyone, though there is terror enough without that notion in my head. My first thought as I fall is, *I'll be in trouble for this one.*

After that, panic and a torrent of new sensations: surprising cold, salt, the bubbling heaviness of the water, the burning of my sinuses. The current, deceptive in its force, moves me almost immediately to the underside of the bowrider, and my hands push against the smooth white shell in hopes of pushing through, back up into the boat where I belong, where my family and a thorough scolding, no doubt, await me.

The light penetrates in places, and my eyes are drawn against my will to diffuse beams that shine like a spotlight, almost to the bottom where great perennial trees—pine or cedar, perhaps—still stand upright, leafless and dead as though frozen in a deep green winter, collapsed into the waters during the making of the artificial bay.

I have a fraction of a moment to speculate on what might lurk there, in the haunted dark beneath those trees, before my body says *breathe.* I know it isn't a good idea, but the body insists, so I breathe. Salt water enters my lungs, and like the screen of my grandparents' elderly TV set, my consciousness flickers and fades, compresses into a weak gray dot in the center of my forehead, then blinks out entirely.

My house was the last on a street that ended in a sharp corner obscured by a tall row of lilac shrubs. Winter had stripped them down to their bare branches, but they were still sufficient to obscure the road behind. I gave it no thought. At any other time of day, I'd have been more cautious. I'd have watched for the glow of approaching lights in the haze. I'd have waited a moment longer, or so I would tell myself after.

The steering wheel was so cold that it hurt to keep my hands on it. I just wanted the drive to be over. Once I was at work I could lose myself, if only for a few hours, in my daydreams. In little scraps of stories I would never find a way to write. The hospital, for all its tedium and chaos, allowed me that much: enough solitude, in those early morning hours, to ponder my internal landscape. The job called for a good deal of walking around, thankfully, which kept me free to imagine, no matter how little hope I had in ever completing a project.

I wanted desperately to write. I dreamed about it. I scribbled notes for potential epic novels on brightly colored sticky notes in hopes of breaking through my own defeatism and into the gilded halls of Writing Process that had thus far eluded me. I wanted a big fat novel of my own that housed powerful, provocative themes and compelling characters. I wanted my name on the front. It seemed impossible, but I wanted it anyway. It would propel me out of my sad circumstances and into literary history, where I hoped I belonged. But my mind seemed incapable of deciphering the map that had been drawn out for me, supposedly, in a high school English class.

Study hard. Read everything and write every day. Stick with it. You can be anything you set your mind to. The words had meant so little when I'd first heard them. Now they felt like mockery. I hated that I had retained them. I wished I could forget them completely, like so much of that time. *Let it die*, I said to my brain, *and use the space for something more lucrative and less depressing.*

It was January the twenty-third—National Rhubarb Pie Day, my computer had reminded me when I got out of bed. I don't know how to make rhubarb pie, or any other pie. Baking is a science of patience, of which I have little. But I had promised to call my grandmother and write down her recipe for a coworker. It seemed pointless in the age of virtually limitless information at the click of a mouse. *Just Google "rhubarb pie," Belinda. You'll be inundated with every pie recipe known to man, so many fucking pie recipes, conflicting and varying in level of skill, that you'll never find your way out.* But sure, I'd call my grandmother. It was probably an overdue phone call anyway, because I was awful at keeping in touch.

My family didn't know about L.A. I had gone to great lengths to keep them in the dark about it, leaving my boring college town in secret two years earlier, literally in the middle of the night, telling almost no one as I left with friends I didn't really know all that well for the vaguely defined life I'd always wanted.

Los Angeles had been immensely fun at first. I could see the Ferris wheel from *Lost Boys* from my street, and a quarter mile to the west was the ocean. There were palm trees, and the city smelled like sand and sun and money, not loneliness and boredom and cow shit like the place I grew up in. Everyone I met wanted to be an actor, a tattoo artist, a late-night talk show host, a model. I didn't tell them about my writing, now limited to the odd alcohol-fueled rant in a tattered, wine-stained notebook left over from college. The mirror world beneath the ocean had rejected my form, the dense collection of parts that composed my body. It had no place there, where air was replaced by water and darkness illuminated light. Any hope of a writing career, the world of the writer, had become similarly impossible to attain. Another upside-down world I didn't know how to reach.

My expensive and extensive cocaine habit didn't help either. I pretended like it was just a party favor, a weekend pastime, and not my breakfast most mornings. When burnout sent me back to Oregon, out of patience with myself and my futile quest for identity, that habit eventually dwindled and died altogether, due to finances rather than any dogged determination to be better.

Out of the driveway, into the empty street. What would I say to my grandmother? *Everyone still alive? I need to know pie things.*

A flash of light, but no screech of slammed-upon brakes. My thought, as my neighbor's car plowed into the side of my own, was: *I almost called out sick.*

→→ ⬧≣⬧ →→

A solidification of things, black and soundless. The liquid in which I am submerged is hardening—into ice, or glass, or something else that I have no words for. The rushing of the water is gone, as is the fear I felt just seconds ago. I can almost touch down on it, on *something*, almost a surface on which to land with hands and knees as I sink slowly down.

Another flash as headlights shattered. The other car was now merged, violently and instantly, with my own in an awkward, boxy yin-yang of red and green paint, careless angles of broken glass and metal, spirals of steam escaping briefly from still-running engines only to be eaten by the freezing fog. The force of the impact spun my car in a semicircle, a violent little dance that ended with a second, lesser collision. Our vehicles were conjoined now, a singular organism, right sides touching but aimed in opposite directions.

All of it—so complex in execution—happened in the span of a single second, in less time than it takes to breathe in, or out. As time resumed its regular flow I became aware that I'd been propelled into my own steering wheel. My head rested there, awkwardly. My neck was twisted at an angle that should have been painful but wasn't. I pulled myself away, and my breath fogged in the ice air that seeped in from the shattered rear windows.

Silence, except for the humming car engines clinging to life. The collision seemed to have pushed everything else away. Lights blinked into existence; I couldn't tell whether they were real or not. My head rang, filled to bursting with a mechanical, musical whine. The lights blinked on closer now, and I recognized them as porch lights, blazing to life earlier than usual. Beyond my injured car: the distorted sounds of human voices murmuring behind walls and windows, barking dogs, the shredding-paper sound of cars passing on the frozen main road a block away, driving on without slowing or stopping. The darkness and trees had hidden us. They couldn't see what had just happened.

I recognized the nearest orange glow as the light from my own house, and I remembered that all of this had happened mere feet from the place I called home. No one opened the front door. They hadn't been disturbed. Their bedroom was on the other side of the house, facing a different street, much quieter, not compromised like this one. I could die in this street, just feet from my bed, and they wouldn't know until the sun exposed the destruction in an hour or so.

You are alive. And nothing hurts. Maybe it isn't as bad as it seems.

I pulled myself upright, or close to it, and I almost laughed at how delusional my own internal dialogue sounded. Something was definitely not right. My senses were off. Even the smell of wood smoke in the air seemed muted in a way I can't explain. The air was sticky on my skin. My heart, drumming away inside me, felt remote.

It's shock. You know it. Was that my own voice? Someone else was running the show now. I was a spectator in the body that had been mine just a few moments earlier.

I'd seen it in other people at the hospital, this behavior. Strange, unexpected calm in their eyes as they waited in the ER lobby, bloody and visibly injured to the point of requiring immediate medical attention. Was this how they felt?

Nothing seemed real, and this thing that had just happened didn't matter as much as it should have.

⊷ ⊷ ⋈✧⋈ ⊶ ⊶

And then, as the water leaves my lungs and stomach, as my heart resumes normal function, the hardening is shattered, breaking away as if struck by some invisible shockwave. I am awake, very much awake and vomiting water, chest and eyes burning, surrounded by people and familiar voices, ashamed and more frightened than I was when the water had briefly consumed me.

⊷ ⊷ ⋈✧⋈ ⊶ ⊶

Raised voices outside. Flashlight beam in fog.

Images from television screens passed through my mind's eye, cars exploding in exaggerated billows of flame and glass. *Get out.*

I pulled myself from the driver's seat. The cold was less cold now, not really cold at all. My car was destroyed, largely, and clearly undriveable. Somewhere in my brain I recognized the car that struck me as our next-door neighbor's strawberry-red Volvo.

Suzanne.

That was her name. The friendly-if-reserved neighbor who'd planted way too many sunflowers in her tiny backyard.

She was still in her car, the front of which was now scrunched up like a rotting accordion alongside mine. She was just sitting there. Her hands were still clamped on the steering wheel. She stared at me with glassy, empty eyes. Some voice in what used to be me said that I should be angry—outraged, in fact. She always blew by in that car, way too fast for where we lived. There were children there. Sure, they never played in the street, but they could.

She didn't hurt the children, she hurt you.

But I wasn't hurt. My car was, but it was just a box that took me places. I knew I was in shock, or something like it. No pain, though. *No permanent damage.*

"You okay?" A male voice. Fatherly. His name was Jim. A volunteer firefighter. He lived just down the street; we could make eye contact from our kitchen windows. Of course he showed up first.

No answer came out, because I didn't know. It was supposed to be freezing, though I couldn't feel it. It was still dark outside. I thought I might be numb from head to toe and I might be dying, but nothing hurt so far. No words would form in my brain, or my throat, or wherever words come from. I could hear my father's voice. *Son, what the fuck is all of this?*

I turned away from Suzanne, sitting so still she might as well have been a Suzanne-shaped mannequin. She seemed well enough, though possibly catatonic, or maybe dead with her eyes wide open.

My face came into full view by way of Jim's flashlight and he stopped moving, stopped fussing around the wreckage. He winced. From looking at me.

That can't be good.

Forming thoughts was difficult. I couldn't form enough words to give him some sign that I was still there, in my own head, in possession of the wits that remained available to me. The only thing that made sense was to get back in the car, to find out why he had reacted the way he did on seeing me. I should have waited for help, but I didn't want to. Nothing hurt. He was overreacting.

"Wait, wait," Jim said, but he made no move to stop me. *He's trained*, I thought. He knew better than to do anything on his own, without paramedic supervision.

In the rearview mirror I can see that the left half of my face was now what a dermatologist, a reconstructive surgeon, or literally anyone with eyes and a vague sense of what other humans look like, would call a "problem area." A solid, blood-black line had been carved down, from forehead to cheek. A crescent-shaped tear in my skin had worked around the outside edge of my left eye, exposing the fragile ridge of bone just underneath. The two lines met in a mangle of flesh and blood on my left cheekbone, a bloody star, exploding into existence an inch below my eye.

My right eyelid, too, was torn slightly at the bottom. In the gloom of fractured headlights and a sweeping flashlight beam I appeared to be weeping blood from both eyes like something out of an Anne Rice novel.

It ran down my face and neck, onto the collar of my scrubs, inky brown against blue. I laughed out loud—a strange, reverse-recording sound—to think that I hadn't noticed it already. Oh, how it must have looked to my rescuers—like I was out of my mind, or brain-damaged, but I couldn't stop laughing. The whole scene just seemed ridiculous.

"You'll be fine," Jim said through the window, but when he spoke I saw my dad. "You're okay."

His hand gently gripped my arm; I jerked it away.

Suzanne, at last, exited her vehicle. She looked at me and made a face similar to Jim's, mute shock mingling with guilt and other things I couldn't find the strength to puzzle out. She collapsed into a loud, tearful panic. *How dramatic*. She looked almost comical from the mascara stains running down her bony cheeks, from the dragon-gouts of fog breath tinted orange-red from cracked brake lights. I stayed seated in my poor, ruined car. *It's warmer in here*, the voice said, but I couldn't feel it if it was.

Paramedics came down the street, weaving from side to side to avoid parked cars, lights flashing red and white and blue, but with no siren to accompany. A fire truck came, amusingly large for the size of the street, sirens blaring unnecessarily but with no flashing lights. Neighbors came to their front porches and living room windows in wrinkled pajamas and bathrobes to witness what had now become a spectacle. My roommates came, at last, frantic and barking orders at emergency workers. Dogs came, too, and children.

Don't look at me. Don't let the children see. I'm fine—just gross and dizzy.

"Sir, can we help you get out? Need to look at ya." Kindly, like Jim. Paramedic woman. A 1950s-diner-waitress accent. Her voice said she had children of her own.

"I'll get out when Suzanne stops screaming," someone inside me said, someone in possession of my speaking organs.

The woman laughed a little.

"Honey, it doesn't seem like she plans to stop anytime soon."

I laughed back. Too loud. The motion of it almost hurt, and the woman signaled into the dancing lights for help.

Finally, Jim returned. Jim, whom I'd never spoken to before, removed me from the car. I couldn't feel his hand on my wrist, or his arm around my waist as he tugged me out, swiftly but gently, a broken, bloody thing now on display for the world to gawk at.

I had just wanted to go to work.

You never want to go to work.

132

The fishing trip is cancelled, of course. We rush back to shore, shouts of "injured kid" and "emergency" announcing us as we reach the docks. And then on to the nearest hospital. Brain, blood, ears, lungs are examined for damage, for abnormality. I am made to walk in a straight line like a suspected drunk driver. I blow into strange blue ribbed tubes with sputtering machines attached to the other end.

One doctor in particular comes repeatedly, always with sugarless candy, asking me to follow his pen, read a few sentences from a book about airplanes, tell him the names and types of all my pets.

"Very good. Very good." Over and over he says it, writing notes on yellow paper, never looking at me directly. He smells of stale coffee, and I am unnerved by the long puffy scars on his face.

"War scars," my grandmother says. "Don't stare."

I spent my days sequestered in my bedroom at the top of stairs like a modern Quasimodo because the five-year-old I lived with would explode into horrified tears at the sight of me. The blood vessels in my right eye remained ruptured for several months after the accident, changing the color from vaguely hazel to terrifying witch-green, staring out from a pool of bright red where white sclera used to be. The bruising and swelling, too, would take forever to fade, and thoughts of the Batman villain Two-Face came to mind every time I caught myself in a reflection.

I dripped with despair at the thought of dying alone—a near-certainty now that I was so permanently disfigured. I imagined living in an upstairs loft with blacked-out windows and nineteen different locks on the door that would click and clank in a rhythm that only I knew, every time the door needed opening, which would of course be rare. I'd do whatever recluses do, and then one day I would die in that loft. They wouldn't find me for a month, when the smell would at last reach the outside world I had abandoned so many years prior.

I did recover, with few enough scars to complain about. I would be told that only I could see them, but I would never fully buy that. Jim was right; I was indeed fine, after all, though broken cars and shattering glass would haunt my dreams for the remainder of the year and half of the next. My jaw and my neck ached constantly, and I feared that the pain and the sound of car windows exploding would never leave me.

Suzanne would apologize ad nauseum. She would drop by sporadically, confusing the entire household with her double-ring of the doorbell and with her strange gifts of fresh-baked bread, peach or apple or huckleberry pie, handmade Christmas tree ornaments, oddly woven cat toys that my cat would stare at blankly and then disregard forever.

⊷ ⊨◊⊟ ⊶

No permanent damage, the doctor's final statement says. Relatives give me little gifts, hug and kiss me and ruffle my hair. They no doubt blame me for being spoiled and untrained. They say, "Be better next time," like I know what that means.

My grandparents waste no time enrolling me in swimming lessons, but I have no intention of revisiting the treacherous world beneath the waves, to navigate such a fearsome and unwelcoming place.

The mirror world was a figment, after all, and the truth of what lies on the other side of the waves is murky vastness, unknown, ambivalent to my plight. It would have claimed me without a second thought, that endlessness. It would have watched with indifference as I flailed and sank into the black, never to be found.

A Detour

When I learn that my brother has died, the first thing that comes to my mind is the lighthouse.

It isn't too far out of the way, just a right turn instead of a left once the ocean is in sight. The trip was initially planned as a fun mini-vacation: leave town, drive west to the Oregon coast and then south to meet up with my husband, who is working on a film set. I'd come and stay with him in the house that his department has rented out, with the magnificent ocean overlook. I would write while he worked. I could walk around Bandon, or find a suitable coffee shop somewhere. Or a bar. Tourist things, but in an artistic, "emerging author" way.

I'm not a tourist, I said to no one, because no one cared. *I was born in this state. I've been coming here all my life.* And then I googled "best fish and chips in Bandon" like every other tourist. And then my brother, James, called me from the front yard of our other brother, Dane's house, with Dane's body still inside.

The standard questions immediately sprang forth, most of them too sad to explore fully, but impossible not to ask. Was it in his sleep, or was he awake when it happened? Did he know he was dying? I had texted with Dane two days before. He was writing a comic book, and I offered to help with the dialogue, though I'm terrible with dialogue. It would never be finished. The day after, I sent him a meme about a dating site for methamphetamine users, joking that we were probably related to a few of them. He had always responded to my messages promptly, but not this time. "I'M NOT A ROLE MODEL," I texted. All caps. No response to that either. I assumed that he wasn't in the mood for my juvenile humor or that he was simply busy, but he was already dead, alone in his bed.

We never spent a single night in the same house together, my brother and I. We shared only one parent in common—our errant father—and when Dane's mother divorced him, Dane and James were removed, almost absolutely with the exception of painfully awkward holidays. They lived mere miles from my own home but in essence were a world away.

We never had a chance to be proper siblings. I always told myself there would be time to fix it, like everyone always does with every last fucking thing until Death says, "Yeah, right." Then we're shocked and ashamed and heartbroken at how lazy and stupid and careless we've been, like we're the first to experience it. Like no one ever warned us.

The lighthouse sits on a tall outcropping of earth and coastal rock, like lighthouses probably should if they want to do their job well. If you know where to look, there's a path that leads through a stretch of barbed-wire fence obscured by bushes, up and over a small rounded hill at the top, past the lightkeeper's house and behind the actual lighthouse, to a tiny ledge of grass where you can sit and stare out across the infinite roll and twist of the Pacific Ocean. No one can see you there. I doubt many people know about it.

I found it many years ago, with friends I no longer have, on a coast trip that was supposed to last for one day and turned into three. We camped on a beach, cooked vegan hot dogs over coals, smoked cheap brown weed, drank box wine and peppermint schnapps (which I do not recommend). We hiked around the forests of the coast in search of nothing in particular. On the final day of the trip, we found the secret cliffs.

I returned there alone the following year. I was in a bad place and briefly considered throwing myself off of that beautiful cliff into the ocean below, where no one would ever find me. Or if they did, if my body washed ashore in the days following, nobody would know *why* I had done it. Was I murdered? Did I have dark secrets?

No one would ever know.

Obviously my determination to jump was weak, but at least my sense of drama was strong. I was still quite young but had experienced my first real taste of failure both in relationships and general "success"— meaning money, of course, or the lack of it. In retrospect, I wasn't doing all that badly, but tell that to any broke and heartbroken twenty-one-year-old and see how they react.

Dane was heavy from as early as second grade. His excessive weight was a problem all through his life, an impairment to the point of disability. Our grandparents blamed everything from genetics to "glandular problems" to a psychological disorder. He had been working for over a year to get better, taking laborious steps toward improving his cardiovascular health by losing weight, being more active, changing his diet and overall psychological state. Two more months and he would have been cleared by his physician for a gastric bypass, a procedure that might have changed his life.

I'm so fucking ready to be happy, he told me.

We believed it, his friends and family. We were ready too.

The lack of fellow drivers on the road makes the journey surreal, like driving through time, through my own past, or future, or perhaps out of the line of time altogether and into an alien landscape in which everything looks normal but clearly isn't. I don't feel like myself, after taking the turn toward the lighthouse. I hover, slightly out of body, as the rest of me drives to a place I barely remember from decades prior.

I hike up the winding trail to the lighthouse. Wind burns my ears and lips, but I will only feel it later. On the lighthouse cliffs, on the mostly obscured fence, is a metal sign, blue paint flaking away to rust from years of ocean air. It urges me—in white letters, all caps—to consider the consequences, the finality and tragedy to the world left behind, of jumping from the cliffs. This is followed by a hotline number for crisis counseling. The sign wasn't there last time. I assume someone must have jumped off in the many years between my visits.

I climb through the barbed wire. I have no intention of jumping, not this time, but the little sign doesn't know that. Its only purpose is to help. Some of its remaining white paint flakes off as it rattles against its post, reminding me of consequences and help only a phone call away.

Save your paint, I tell it. *I'm okay.*

I think Dane's chronic overeating stemmed from a need for comfort from the harshness of the world around him. Sensitive and artistically inclined, he cried easily as a child, sometimes at things that seemed innocuous: an excited calf playing in a field, a Heart song playing on the radio. He enjoyed conversations about deep topics that most others would avoid. He couldn't tune out the sadness, the horrors of life on Earth like most people can. It made him retreat and seek comfort in food. I understand how it feels to wish for a better life, a better existence, and

137

not know how to begin attaining it. Add it to the list of things I wish I'd told him.

The tiny half shell of sea grass and rock is exactly as I remembered it: perfectly out of view, accessible only if you know where to climb. Looking out, only ocean, thin sunlight, bored seagulls and cormorants floating in the wind, the broken black maw of rocks far below, where at least one person ended their time in the world.

I am alone, damp salt wind stinging my skin, the Pacific roaring, away from everyone. No one knows I am here. I left my phone in the car. I haven't brought a book. There is nothing to do but sit, and mourn, and I haven't a clue how to do it.

It is beautiful, to be sure, sitting alone on an ocean cliff like this one, facing the sea, the edge of the world. Irritatingly, embarrassingly beautiful. Like I've stepped into a bad calendar, the kind you might find in some lonely office cubicle next to a yellowed outdated emergency phone number list. Like there should be some trite inspirational quote floating over my head in elaborate, loopy cursive white letters over a pastel ocean sunrise: *You have to look through the rain to see the rainbow.*

Ugh.

Why am I here? My brother never saw this place. Maybe I just want to be alone and this place represents the most alone I can be in the world. Maybe this place was made for that feeling, one I've cultivated unwittingly through years and years of absence. Maybe I deserve to be alone. Maybe I want to see the cliffs and the ocean below, to remember what it is like to come close to death.

We're all close to Death, always right up next to it, some lingering "goth kid" version of me says from inside. I roll my eyes at his dramatic tone, his capitalization of the word "death." But it's true. I can see to the inevitable end now. I knew it was there. I'm not all that afraid of it. *Just not yet*, everyone ever has said, and I say it now too.

Again I register how this place looks just like it did when I came here before. Time seems unwilling to touch it. Instead, she just sits here in silence with the birds and the pale sun, dangling her feet over the edge. She neglects me too, now, for a moment. Unconcerned, she loses sight of me as I sit here, motionless and aimless at the edge of the world. My past and my future lock eyes and collide. Me on a cliff in the middle.

Maybe I've been sitting here since the first time, since I first found the place. Maybe I was always here when I needed to be elsewhere, when my loved ones wondered after me and wished I was with them and died alone. My brother wasn't the first, I recall, and a long slug of

138

bitter, syrupy guilt slides down my gullet. I have a habit of not being there, of being gone. I left my family a long time ago and I never really came back.

Gail was the "cool aunt," too kindhearted for her own good. She died like my brother: suddenly, alone in her room. My grandmother found her in the morning, cold to the touch and stiff with rigor mortis. *Come quick*, she told my father. *I think Gail is dead.* Her life seemed sad as soon as it ended, or maybe it was before and we simply chose to overlook it in hopes of some grand revival from her, some late-in-life change for the better.

My grandfather's body counted down in labored breaths and slowing heartbeats to the morning on which he exited the world, having reached, after years of suffering, a critical mass of failed organs and metastatic blood. I had said goodbye less a week before, almost like nothing was wrong, like he'd recover after the cancer had run its course, like the next time I came home he'd be tooling around in the garden, complacently panting dog at his side, swearing at tomato plants, humming some old country music song, making my grandmother blush through the kitchen window with some off-color joke as she stood inside, peeling carrots over the sink for dinner.

Even my beloved cat, my only friend when I came to Portland, who'd made the journey with me, was lost to a malfunction of the kidneys that struck when I left him alone overnight. Busy living, I had failed to notice his decline until, as though the years with him prior had been only a lightning strike of happy memory, he was lying limp in my arms.

I'm so bad at being there. I'm naturally distant. My parents are too—another gift from them. We're all better from far away, personified watercolor paintings that, from across the room, seem lovely, intriguing and vibrant and possessed of great depth. Up close, an absolute mess: overly, unnecessarily complicated, confusing, haphazardly composed.

I remember the last time I ever saw Dane in person. He had reached out to me, after years of unintentional distance created by the living of one's life, by time. He wrote to me, told me he was happy I'd escaped the small-town existence that clearly wasn't for me. He and a friend were coming to Portland for a concert, and he wanted to meet my new husband. He was the first (and, to date, the only) member of my father's family to do so.

We met him at a bar in northwest Portland. "My god," he said as we walked in. "You look exactly the same. Is it voodoo or Botox?"

My husband was shocked, I think, at his size, how it made him stand out so completely. He was drinking a beer, which made him seem like an adult to me, suddenly, as if he'd been a child still, until that moment, until my mind caught up with the rules of time, with the many years that had passed since we'd set eyes on each other.

We moved outside, to a covered patio with pool tables, where he seemed less nervous, less awkward. He was effortlessly friendly with my husband. They laughed heartily at my expense almost immediately, Dane regaling my husband with stories about me as a horrible trickster child, as a sour-faced teenager bedecked in oversized black draperies I called "clothes" and smudged Halloween makeup, as the present older sibling I never really was.

We stayed for hours, laughing and drinking. I drank way more than I should have in the middle of my workweek: beer at first, then gin, then tequila. I felt like I was dying the next morning, but it was worth it. I would never see him again.

When we left, he hugged me and said, "You did good, brother." I don't remember what I said back, but I recall the sound of my voice coming near to breaking with the weight of all the times I should have helped him, encouraged him, consoled him, and hadn't.

My dead brother doesn't feel dead enough to mourn, but he is. Later there will be a memorial on the ocean. His ashes will be spilt off the back of a boat into the turbulent bay, as requested in the will we never expected to read or need so soon. The messages I sent him will never be answered. His stories will remain unwritten, unfinished. My kindhearted brother, who in no way deserved to die young and alone, will become an oily gray slick in the ocean, and then nothing. He's somewhere else now, or nowhere, or everywhere.

I hope it's that one. Everywhere.

Time takes notice of me, finally. Smirks at me. Corrects the malfunction, adjusts her flowing skirts, and snaps the window shut.

I'm freezing on that cliff, absolutely freezing. How long have I been here? My husband, if I linger here too much longer, will wonder where I am. He will worry. He expects me soon at his rented house in Bandon. He waits there with dinner and wine and love—the spoils of the life I built while I was gone.

The trail down to my car seems longer than it was on the way up. The journey seems to take years instead of hours. My husband—my happiness—is here, in the *now*, in the present that I almost lost sight of on that cliff, only an hour's drive to the south along the foggy coast. For him, I won't be gone. I've already spent too much time alone.

How to Go Home Again

"**W**hat's not to write about?" my husband says. "You were a gay goth kid on a farm in a tiny Oregon town with missing parents. Isn't that enough to start with, at least?"

Good point.

It's a grueling process, though. It's painful sometimes, to form words and sentences and paragraphs that make sense to anyone other than me, but Ursula said keep writing, and my writing instructor says it in myriad ways, even when she wants me to rewrite the whole fucking thing. Now my husband says it too—the goofy, lanky Wisconsin boy, in mannerism and temperament reminiscent of a domesticated wolf-dog, who fixes the things in my head that have been "not fixed" for so long that I forgot about them entirely, who loves me more than I deserve on most days.

→•→ ᙓ◆ᙓ →•→

I found my new home with him, but I still long, at times, for the original. Not the slowly crumbling house that borders the nearly dead town I grew up in, but the feeling of "home" that I gave up—the feeling of safety and stability that everyone craves, the feeling that everything is okay, or will be, or doesn't need to be. I long for who I used to be, and who they used to be. I long for the peace of not having to worry and the peace of not knowing. I long for simplicity in a life of complications and convolutions. I know I'm not special in this, but that knowledge doesn't lessen the pangs of wishing that things could have been better for me and my somewhat-estranged family who call only when someone dies or someone is about to. I'm no better; I don't call either.

Even when the truth of my childhood was finally revealed, when my mother could no longer keep the secret in check, even after I processed the feelings of betrayal and loss that inevitably followed, I wished I could have it back.

I wished for it after Los Angeles. As I flew into the Eugene airport, some piece of me was expecting something grand on arrival: a gaudy handmade "Welcome Home" sign, a crowd of familiar faces who had never been so happy to see me again, a sense of "full circle" completed by my long-awaited return. But the plane landed unceremoniously, and none of those things were real. Instead, as expected, my grandmother and aunt sat nervously in the terminal, in magenta and seafoam sweaters, their purses held close since thieves lurk at every turn, while I shuffled toward them like the walking dead—the walking dead of the 1950s, who seemed like no threat at all compared with today's speedier zombies.

They'd driven eighty miles in the snow to collect me, but I was still tempted to dodge them and slink into the bar, spend my remaining cash on morning booze and just fade out of the world into calm, lukewarm nothingness. I was sober, and desperately wished I wasn't even though it was ten in the morning. But they could already see me, and anyway, I didn't have enough money left to get as drunk as I would have liked.

I'd crashed and burned, left the dream of all the things I planned to succeed at once my life in L.A. was "stabilized." I'd failed utterly at everything. I'd come home.

"You're so skinny!" My aunt leaned in to embrace me. She still wore the same perfume. I'd forgotten how it smelled, though a thousand memories stored away in my brain sparked to life at the vague flower-vanilla scent. I stiffened instinctively at the hug, told myself that this was familiar and should be a comfort after the year I'd had. It was January. I'd missed Christmas, and Thanksgiving, and whatever else took place in the year prior.

"We can get some breakfast on the way home if you want," my grandmother chimed in, kindly brown eyes darting back and forth from passerby to exit. "You still like pancakes, right?" She was still always fixing, always helping, always finding the jewel in the bucket of shit. I hadn't eaten breakfast in months, and her use of the word "home" was both foreign to me and a silent slap in the face. The place she referred to was not my home anymore, try as I might to return. It was just the only place I had left to go.

My bedroom was the shiny, garish green I remembered. The trim was pale blue, a horrible combination chosen for that reason—deliberately mismatching things for dramatic or comedic effect. It seemed like an emerald-tone prison now, like someone else's memory, and I wished I had chosen any other color. Better yet, I wished I had let someone else choose for me, a wish that spread, infectious, to most other areas of my life as I lay awake in my childhood bed rehashing the series of terrible choices and equally terrible lack of them that had landed me squarely, miserably back where I started. "Why didn't I?" permeated my skull. Why didn't I what? Live more? Dream more realistically? Make more money? Fall in line easier? Do better at things I never wanted in the first place?

Relatives and family friends stopped by to welcome me home. My grandmother offered to cook the meals I loved when I was ten. I accepted, and tried to seem excited, but I could only keep up the façade for the briefest of interactions, like holding your breath after climbing a hill or tensing the muscle you've been lifting with all day. It made me shaky and angry, and I retreated to my ugly bedchamber to weep softly and smoke out the window like I had been chastised for so many times my old life.

The kindness surrounding me seemed like mockery. Their vastly overabundant kindness had made me soft, complacent. Their willingness to do everything for me and take care of me and placate me in every possible way had created a deficit of ambition, a general lack of drive to work hard or succeed. It burned now, and I found myself angry at them and unable to explain why. They wouldn't have understood if I had berated them for loving me, even if they loved me too much and it ruined me.

This was not home anymore. The memories, though mostly good, were just that. I'd already left, and I knew the day I did, as the house shrank and disappeared in my rearview mirror, as I took the freeway exit south, that I wouldn't come back.

I'd already left, so leaving again was easy, though the sadness my grandmother was clearly masking was both a stab in the throat and the final straw that sent me fleeing for a new city, for one more try at a life I actually wanted to live. I didn't know how to try very hard, but whatever effort I might muster would beat the slow death of small-town existence. Maybe that's where my determined fire had been hiding all those years: in the terror of being trapped in a life I hated, nauseating "Top 40" country music always playing in the background while I got fat with the wife I didn't know how to talk to and tried my hardest to avoid the kids I'd never wanted in the first place.

Instead I found, in the city my family (in their eyes) had lost me to, my love, after years of disastrous, volatile relationship fails. I found him and it was nothing like I'd been told—no ringing bells or perfect days—but he did, in a sense, complete me. It would never have, for my family, the same shine as if I'd stayed in Riddle, married some girl, bought some house, produced some grandkids to be fawned over and spoiled. My gay city husband only serves to distance me from the people who raised me, but it doesn't matter. I was never meant to stay.

⊷⊷ ⊠✦⊠ ⊶⊶

I'm almost forty, and I have nothing left to lose. So I say fuck it and write more. My closet is full of notebooks, full in turn with scribblings and half-finished ideas for films and novels and short stories, general thoughts on the world. My history, sloppy and insecure and malformed, but it's there. I never really stopped, even when I couldn't bear the sight of my own thoughts on paper, when everything I wrote seemed like a shallow, sad mimicry of something already done far better than I'd ever do it.

I have a lifetime of weird things to write about. My life seemed too ordinary to ever be worthy of the page, but maybe the magic is in the telling. Ursula Le Guin said it, standing diminutively onstage. She asked me to keep writing as she signed my book that summer night. She said the world needs more writers. It seems laughably corny if I say it out loud, but I kept those words like she'd never said them to anyone else. I use them now to keep going, as I slowly write my life out: its secrets, its revelations, its failings, its joys and pains. It might not be an epic, an award-winning bestseller, but I've already started and now it has to have an ending.

Maybe this is where you find your way back, I tell myself. It's not in traveling there. It's not in reconnecting or phone calls or in the few objects you've held on to from that time. It's in the words you write about the place you once called home. It's in the feel, the descriptions, good and bad and indifferent alike, of the people. This is what you're good at; it might be the only thing. This is the piece that was missing for so long.

144

Maybe your family would have preferred that you stay, rather than write a biased account of them all that isn't always flattering, that is subject to distortions of memory and emotion and time. Maybe they missed you more than they ever said. It would make sense, given your inability to emote verbally; maybe you're more a product of the family you abandoned than you're willing to admit.

But maybe it was they who, however inadvertently, shaped you into this thing that now sits at a desk on the other end of time, trying to give life to these memories, these old stories that are largely lost and forgotten, that only you now recall. Maybe this is how you say, "Thank you" and "I'm sorry" and "I love you too." Maybe this, ultimately, is all you have to give.

Acknowledgments

This collection would not be possible without the assistance of so many wonderful humans.

Thank you to my mother and father, my brothers, my aunts and uncles and cousins, to my in-laws of the Pacyna and Gover variety, and also to my Portland family. I am profoundly grateful for all of you.

Thank you to Justin Daniels, Tabitha Trosen, Bridget Larrabee, Levi Sheppard, Adrienne Stone, Nate Pacyna, Travis D'Ambrogi, and Max "Potato Salad" Volk for creating my fantastic book trailer, and for one of the most enjoyable evenings in recent memory. Special thanks to Justin for throwing the idea my way in the first place, for years of friendship and laughs, and for harassing me incessantly until I finally agreed to move to Portland. I'm so glad you did.

Thanks to Leanne Sisco-King, Dena Cooper Ganieany, and Delaine Barnes for your help with facts and time lines and for your general encouragement and support of this project.

Thanks to Malika Semper for the celestial wisdom, for being a dear friend for so very long, and for being one of the funniest gals around.

Thank you to Harper Quinn, Alley Pezanoski-Browne, and everyone at IPRC for facilitating the early seed of collected writings that would eventually become this book.

Thank you to my friend and instructor: the wise, hilarious, incomparable Margaret Malone. Your guidance has been transformative. Thank you for helping me to find the happiness in my writing and for reminding me to slow down when I'm rushing through a scene like I'm on fire.

Massively heartfelt thanks to my publisher, Cindy Neil, for believing in my work, for your kind words and support throughout this process, and for being so much fun to work with. You have made a dream come true for me here.

Thank you to Rick Louis for the editing expertise. Your miraculous ability to find and refine the point I'm trying to make in my ramblings has made this collection so much more accessible and concise. Thank you also for regulating my excessive swearing and my grievous misuse of semicolons.

For my husband, Nate Pacyna, thank you for your endless love and support. Thank you for the gentle kicks in the ass that keep me going when I feel like jumping ship. Thank you also for being my first reader, my unofficial life coach, my mental health therapist, and my sounding board during the writing of this book (and just in general). You have made me realize that it's never too late to be happy. I'm the luckiest boy in the world for having found you.

To Dane: You are dearly missed. Thank you for your friendship, and for your immeasurably kind heart.

This book is dedicated in part to my mother, Lenae; my grandmother, Wilma; and my aunt Gail—my trio of moms—all of whom have shaped me in ways I'm still discovering. To my mother in particular: I hope I've done our stories justice. I hope that the truths told here can help us both close a few doors and open some new ones. You never really left. I love you.